Grace & Truth

Essays for the Edification of the Saints

Grace & Truth

Essays for the Edification of the Saints

Edited by

Bradley W. Maston

and E Dane Rogers

Published by

True Grace Books

Tacoma, WA | Fort Collins, CO

Grace & Truth: Essays for the Edification of the Saints

True Grace Books, *Vashon, WA*

Published by True Grace Books LLC

Grace & Truth: Essays for the Edification of the Saints / Edited by Bradley W. Maston and E Dane Rogers.

Library of Congress Control Number: 2023911965

ISBN: 978-1-7327779-3-4

1. Bible. 2. Theology. 3. Essays, Theological

Interior design and editing by E Dane Rogers
Cover design by E Dane Rogers

Printed in the United States of America

Table of Contents

Forward

Dr. Maston has done it again by producing an important book. Here he gathered a group of highly endowed writers, pastors and theologians producing a large number of essays for us to reflect on and share with the saints. He has included a group of essays that bring to bear on our community topics necessary to help us grow theologically in areas that seem to be left out of many publications and sermons. It is in this context that this new work by Brad Maston is a welcome contribution. This is a work that seeks to fill in the blanks of all such topics that most pastors neglect to teach or just gloss over in their desire to please the masses. We should not shy away from sound theology and doctrine in a desire to give our audiences what they want and not necessarily what God wants for them to have.

It is my prayer that these essays will be promulgated wide and far to many churches and seminaries so that we are all reminded of their importance to the growth and development of the saints in the evangelical institutions in which we are placed. We have been given a Bible with two testaments comprised of sixty-six books. Each of these essays should cause us to dive deeper into the totality of Scripture and grow to appreciate the depth and extent of the Bible that God has written for us to increasingly enjoy Him. We will realize this appreciation as we explore the light each one of these authors in this work have shined on the Lord's words to us. This whole work is written in an edifying style and I offer a plea for all pastors to engage in an honest evaluation of the depth of their teaching to their congregations in bringing the Word of God to this world. God wants us to know Him in a more meaningful way. This book assists us with that.

Daniel E Woodhead, Ph.D.

Preface

"And do not be conformed to this world, but be transformed by the renewing of your mind, that you may prove what *is* that good and acceptable and perfect will of God." (Romans 12:2)

The renewing of the mind is a centrally important idea in the process of growing in the Christian life. Our worldly and fleshly thoughts are gradually replaced with godly, biblical thoughts by regular examination of the Scripture and consideration of all that God has revealed. Yet, like every task which the Lord gave the church, it is never a solo project. This is a group project. It is not up to any one individual to learn, understand, and explain every aspect of God's perfect word. That task falls to all of us as a body. That is where this book of essays, articles, and bible studies comes into the picture.

This book of essays is designed to offer encouragement on a wide variety of issues. Articles of simple devotion, textual exposition, and theological interest all sit together comfortably and present the reader with a wide variety of topics to challenge and encourage us in our walk with Christ. The balance of these essays, it is hoped, will have something not only to offer every believer, but also to help every believer grow to gain a broader understanding of what it means to walk with Jesus Christ. The exacting theology hound must benefit from the simpler works of pure devotion. The person only interested in practical concerns will benefit from expanding their understanding to see the great importance of deeper consideration of the revelation of God's word. This is how Christians grow: by listening to what other believers have learned and brought back to share. This is teaching. This is what this book of essays is about.

The next purpose of this book is to engage some important issues about which most everyone has an opinion, but few take the time evaluate. The essays that provide such perspectives encourage us to consider things that we may not have considered before. One blessing of studying Christian Theology is that it is the greatest environment in the world for learning. The simple fact that God is always right means that we can easily change our minds whenever we find that our thinking is in contrast with His revelation. A person who has not been challenged in their thinking probably isn't thinking very much. Sadly, we tend to simply recycle the same old thoughts over and over. Treading remembered paths, repeating our old ideas, and hoping that nothing comes from outside to rock the boat. This book is designed to stimulate deeper and more serious thought.

In conclusion, I assert: all theology is practical theology. What we believe about God matters. Those who prayerfully and humbly consider the truth of God's word bring forth insights that will spur us on towards seeing Jesus Christ more clearly. The variety of essays in this book is certainly quite diverse but within that diversity is a single purpose – each essay will challenge the reader to know the Lord better, to respond to His love, and live a life that glorifies God, all by His grace. May God richly bless you as you read these essays.

The Abiding Life

By Randy Peterman

Christianity is full of all sorts of people who are floundering and yet there are other people who are growing. All under one banner as the church. Many Christians are unable to tell which category they're under and others cast aspersions when sin enters the public eye. What does the Bible say? How can we tell where we're at? How can we walk confidently in God's truth? The answers to these questions all link back to abiding. What is Abiding?

Houses and Addresses

Upon believing the gospel of Jesus Christ we are indwelt by the Holy Spirit. Many Christians hear that and are rightfully amazed. The ministry of the Holy Spirit continues in the life of the believer in a deeper, empowering way. That is, if we abide. Our relationship is changed from being children of wrath to being children of God, but our fellowship can be richer and growing.

The Greek word μένω, translated 'to abide,' in the English means to dwell, to stay, or to remain. When Jesus was separated from his parents they came back and found him at the temple and he said to Joseph and Mary, "Why is it that you were looking for Me? Did you not know that I had to be in My Father's house?" (cf. Lk. 2:49). Jesus was dwelling with the Father. We'll look more at Christ as an example later. The Holy Spirit indwells us (cf. Rom. 8:26–27; 1 Cor. 2:12–13; Eph. 1:13–14; 2:22; 3:16), He abides in us, and we're called to abide in Him, too! When we dwell, remain, or stay in fellowship with the Godhead we are abiding. Our relationship is sealed because of what Christ did on the cross, but our moment-by-moment fellowship with Them is rooted in the idea of abiding.

Synonyms

Galatians 5:16: Walk by the Spirit

Many people are familiar with the deeds of the flesh and the fruits of the Spirit from Galatians 5, but the earlier verse in the passage tells us, "But I say, walk by the Spirit, and you will not carry out the desire of the flesh." Walking by [the direction of] the Spirit is to have communed or dwelt with the Holy Spirit and listened to His guidance. This doesn't remove our personality from the equation, but it neuters the desires of the flesh. We may go serve the body, or preach the gospel, or make a tough choice in a personal way, but it is by the direction of the Holy Spirit with whom we intimately relate.

Colossians 3:1–3: Setting Our Minds on Things Above

Paul tells us in Colossians 3:1–3 that our address (sometimes called our position) is before God in Christ, but our thinking (sometimes called our condition) is here on earth, where we are to be setting our minds on things above. This idea of setting our minds on things above is to be dwelling mentally on what the Godhead has for us.

Ephesians 5:18–6:17: Filled with the Spirit

This is a long passage to cite, but the nature of being filled by the Spirit impacts the entire body towards learning, listening, worshiping, living together peacefully, and standing together in Christ. How will the believer be imitating God (Eph. 5:1–2)? The believer does so by being filled with the Spirit and living out the abiding life. The Holy Spirit enables us to be listening under, to be serving, and to be thankful in everything.

Hebrews 4: Rest & Drawing Close

In Hebrews 4:1–11 the author tells us to enter God's rest. To willfully set our mental and emotional focus into the place where, spiritually, we have value and access. In verse 16 he tells us that we should be drawing close to God's throne. An opportunity to draw close to the throne of the God of the universe? Are you out of your mind? That could be deadly! Except that it is not. It is a right for those who are righteous. It is where Christ has already identified us through His work on the cross. It is where the Holy Spirit leads us to fellowship and rest.

Moment-By-Moment

The human brain experiences the sense of now as a rolling 2.5 second period of time. The believer is called to be abiding and that can be a real relief, but it can also be discouraging if at some point in time you realize you are not abiding, but instead engaging in the deeds of the flesh. At that point in time the Holy Spirit will be calling for you to rejoin in fellowship. Do it! Don't lean into fleshly guilt and feeling remorse for a prolonged period of time so that God will know you're really sorry. Instead, in that moment, recognize you weren't abiding, and then draw close, set your mind on things above and walk by the Spirit. Done.

While our earthly experience may be distracted, deceived, or disgusting, our heavenly position is assured in grace, hope and love, and so we are to be, moment-by-moment, volitionally engaging in an intimate lovefest with the God of the universe: dwelling, remaining, and staying in God's love and life.

A Moment-By-Moment Life

Ultimately one of the outcomes of our being sanctified is that our life reflects His life. From the outside others will see God's righteousness (cf. Jn. 3:7). It will be summarily called the life of Christ by those observing us. Our fellowship and walking by the Spirit will be a moment-by-moment life where we consider our thoughts and take them captive (2 Cor. 10:5) and renew our minds (Rom. 12:2–3), proving out what the will of God is and living as individuals, a body, and impacting our community and the world.

Old Testament Foundational Principles

It would be unfortunate to not recognize the consistency of God in His plan for humanity to:

1. Be designed in such a way that intimacy with Him is possible
2. Be designed in such a way that the Holy Spirit can interface with us as creator
3. Be known by Him
4. To know Him

Since abiding is fundamentally about fellowship with God, how did He set that up to operate? What principles have been in place since the beginning.

Made in God's Image: Genesis 1:26–27

Since the 6th day of creation God created man distinct from the beasts of the field, the birds of the air, and the fish of the sea. None are described as being made in His image. They reflect His creativity, but they don't express His personhood and spiritual life. God made Adam in His image and likeness. God then interacted with Adam in such a way that Adam would be forced to reconcile a major disparity: he had no female counterpart! Together Adam and Eve walked with the Lord in the garden. Their nakedness did not separate them. They did not deeply understand good and evil. They just walked with God. They dwelt in the garden and God made Himself available to them to have fellowship with the God of the universe. They had one rule: Don't eat the fruit of the tree of the knowledge of good and evil.

Volition – Sin Breaks Relationship: Genesis 3

Upon choosing to eat that fruit, their relationship - which came with the blessing of life and fellowship with God – turned into separation. God came to walk with them and found that they knew good and evil. At this point in time the idea of the 'sin nature' entered the equation. Adam and Eve repent of their sin and believe after a bit of dancing trying to shift the blame from themselves to anyone else and God covers them and sends them out of the garden. The account of Cain and Able in Genesis 4 tells us further about the problems of volition and will. It's worth calling out that Cain was really angry at Able, but since the number of people he had as confidants was very limited Cain tells Able about his frustrations and God's direction to not let sin master him. Then Cain kills him. Pretty wicked, dark, and very much a choice he did not have to make.

Enoch: Genesis 5:21–24

In stark contrast to the murderous brother, we find Enoch as a godly man who walks with God. Enoch's dwelling with God is so remarkable that God appears to take him away so that the natural death as a result of sin is not Enoch's end.

Salvation is by Faith, Faith is by Volition

When we come to the account of Abraham in Genesis 11:26-25:8 we find that Abraham believed God. He had faith. That faith was credited to him as righteousness. It didn't matter that he lied to Pharaoh in Egypt. It didn't matter that he did any number of other knuckleheaded things. He believed and was saved. Belief is not just mental ascent but is volitionally recognizing a truth and then committing to respond to that truth with trust and confidence.

Thinking God's Thoughts After Him – AKA The Law

The Law calls Old Testament saints in Israel to walk by the 613 commands that God put forth in the Pentateuch (the first five books of the Bible). They're instructed to be separated by their social, moral, and spiritual practices from the pagan countries around them. However, as Paul reiterates for us in Romans 4:13: For the promise to Abraham or to his descendants that he would be heir of the world was not through the Law, but through the righteousness of faith. When we recognize the Law's purpose, we see that it was to draw Israel into fellowship based on an already established relationship.

An Established Relationship Means Walking in Fellowship

King David understood the importance of fellowship because he knew that the relationship was secure. When he repented of sin (2

Sam. 11–24) he did so, knowing that God had not moved; rather, he himself had. David boldly approached God not out of arrogance, but out of understanding. David violated the Law through lustfulness, murder, deception, and even through a census. God's mercy was there and defined God's faithful character for David. David knew he was to think God's thoughts after Him, but that doing so was going to deepen their fellowship with God (cf. Psa. 19; 111; 119).

New Testament Foundational Principles

Christ, the Example of Abiding

In John 15 abiding is presented to the disciples where the idea of dwelling with Christ and Christ with the disciples will lead to life, and the Father will bless and grow and dress [prune or lift up] the vines. Christ modeled this concept of abiding by abiding with the Father! He and the Father are one (Jn. 10:30; 17:11, 21) and their dwelling together modeled something that the pharisees did not model. It modeled something that was spiritually pure, and reflected a relationship that Christ prayed for his followers in John 17.

Observations from John 15

We should recognize that Jesus was having a conversation with his disciples that was to teach them a truth they had not properly grasped. They had grown up around the religious leaders and rabbis that had more than likely completely ignored the relationship dynamic that Jesus was teaching about regarding dwelling and oneness. Christ's analogy [it is not an allegory] is to teach the parallels of fellowship due to relationship. The Father is the vinedresser, and that means that He's actively inspecting the way that the branches connect to the vine, Christ. The vinedresser is intentionally doing the best thing for the whole plant including pruning, tying, lifting up, training, and generally doing what is best for the health of that plant. The Greek word translated 'takes away' in the NASB (v. 2a) could also be translated 'lifts up' or 'carries up'. While Christ may very well have wanted to indicate that some branches would be removed and carried up, it is also part of training the branches along the plant to reach the trellis where they will get the most sunshine, support, and therefore produce the most fruit.

The idea of pruning that does come in verse 2b is still not the removal of the branch, but a trimming of the branch so that its energy will be directed to the most important thing: producing fruit.

Christ then tells His disciples that they are already clean (v. 3). That cleanness is due to what God has bestowed, not of the disciples' personal excellence. If you're going to be dwelling, abiding, or connected to the vine, it will be because you are already clean. Verse 4 then draws the comparative parallel of the analogy: dwelling. Just as you are bound by a relationship you must choose to dwell in fellowship.

Christ then makes some declarative statements to His disciples around promises and supernatural outcomes that we should carefully avoid taking on as promises to ourselves. John picks up on the abiding principles in a believer's life and what we can expect in 1 John 3 and 4. The reason we look at the abiding principles in John 15 is because along with John 17 we can see Christ having lived out an absolutely perfect example-filled life of abiding (cf. Jn. 17:6).

Observations from John 17

Often called "The Real Lord's Prayer" by many believers, John 17 records an intimate moment between Jesus and the Father. In this special time of Prayer Christ makes some very powerful statements about who we are and God's intent for us. The beginning of Christ's prayer is rich with theology about the Godhead and who Christ is, but we'll pick up in verse 9: Christ says that His disciples are God's; they are of Him. Then Christ says that the disciples have glorified Him, which is a clear reference to their understanding exactly who Christ was. He wasn't just a rabbi; He was the Son of God. In verse 11 Christ then asks that they be kept in His name so that they can be one like Christ and the Father are one. They know whom their name is in (cf. Eph. 3:14–19). Jumping forward to verse 20 Christ asks on behalf of those who believe because of the accounts of the disciples and later the apostles.

Then Christ once again asks for them to be one as He and the Father are one (vv. 21–22). Are you ready to have your mind blown? Because verse 24 is about being seated in the heavenly places with Christ. Christ prays for the identification of His followers to be with Him where He is. Where is He? With the Father in the heavenlies.

Identification Truths – Position vs. Condition

Paul shocks readers of the New Testament even today by telling them that they are currently dead, buried, resurrected, and seated in the heavenlies with Christ. He does so in Romans 6:3, Ephesians 2:4–6, and Colossians 3:1–3. This concept of being identified with Christ is shocking because Paul writes in the present tense. Believers have used the terms 'positional' and 'conditional' to distinguish between our earthly condition and our heavenly position. When we're joined with Christ in the heavenlies our position and our condition will be unified. Our position in Christ before God is one where – at the point of salvation – we were there with Christ on the cross, we were there with Christ in His death, we were there with Christ in the tomb, we were risen on the 3rd day and we are now seated in the heavenly places with Christ. Our position is sealed by virtue of Christ's work and its being irreversible. Our position is therefore impactful to our condition. Paul's imperatives often flow out of a 'therefore' that is linked to who we are in Christ. This is sometimes called a logical imperative: it is logical that since our position is with Christ in the heavenlies that our condition would reflect that righteousness.

The Ministry of the Holy Spirit

Indwelt, Filled, and Empowered by the Holy Spirit

The Indwelling

In Romans 5:5, 8:9, 1 Corinthians 2:12–13 and 3:16, we see that as New Testament saints we are indwelt by the Holy Spirit. This is why we can walk by the Spirit and bear spiritual fruit instead of the deeds of the flesh. When we entangle ourselves with carnal motives rather than our relationship with God through the Holy Spirit, we don't bear fruit. But when we abide, or as Paul says, "walk by the Spirit," we manifest the life of Christ, the fruit of the Spirit, and the love of the Father.

The Filling

Ephesians 5:18 is a pivotal verse within the book of Ephesians. As Paul goes into the practical nature of being imitators of God (Eph. 5:1) he makes his way into how it is done. That is by being filled and fulfilled by the Holy Spirit (instead of being drunk). The command to be filled is in the 2nd person passive plural which tells us a lot about what Paul's intent is: as a body of saints, we are to be allowing the Holy Spirit as a corporate vessel to fill us. With that filling as an assumed starting point Paul then goes into how the saints have moved from imitators to agents to loving collaborators.

The Empowering the Fruit

The Holy Spirit motivates and empowers us to do things (cf. Gal. 5:22–23; Eph. 5:9). Coupling this with Paul's describing himself with striving and you've got a lot of energy going into something. We don't all strive all the time, of course, but there may be times when the Holy Spirit moves you to do something through spiritual gifting and you're unstoppable because He's unstoppable. Spiritual gifts aren't about you, but they are absolutely about you being a vessel and the Holy Spirit empowering you within the church body. This is where abiding spreads from the first person (I'm abiding in love and blessing) to the second person (you are loved and blessed through me), and when it does that, it often gets the attention of those who don't believe, and then it moves to the third person (they are loved and blessed – "I want that!") Stated more succinctly: God will move through you, it will impact the body, and everyone else outside of the body is going to take notice.

Rest & Drawing Close to the Throne

In Hebrews chapter 4 we see two key concepts that are part of dwelling with God: First He calls us to diligently enter rest (v. 11) and second, He calls us to draw close to the throne (v. 16). Some will ask the questions already: but how do I rest? How do I draw near to the throne? The answer comes in the concept of abiding. The author of Hebrews led into chapter 4 with an account of the Jews wandering in the wilderness. They were not in a state of rest. They weren't in the promise land. They weren't relying on the Lord at their core, but instead they were complaining and whining and ignoring that the God of the Universe had called them to be free of slavery!

We're called to not only rest in what God has done. That He has redeemed us and called us His own, but also to boldly draw close to the throne of the Father. This idea comes with the concept of willfully resting in what Christ has done:

- He has made us righteous
- He has made us just
- He has made us glorified
- He has bought us with a price
- He was the propitiation so that the Father was satisfied
- He declared us His bride
- He has washed us with the water of the word
- He has removed all sin from before the eternal judgment of the Father

What can be calling you to guilt? Not the Holy Spirit! Draw close to the Father who desires your fellowship since He has established the relationship! Dwell with Him!

Sanctification, Transformation, & Conformation

Sanctification

Abiding is the state we are spiritually and mentally in that God uses for our spiritual growth. We progressively are sanctified from immaturity to maturity (1 Cor. 6:11). We must start as babes, but we don't have to stay there. Sanctification means in its simplest sense: to be set aside. The Lord's life and the Holy Spirit renew our minds and change how we live. Idea by idea. Area by area. Grace upon grace.

As we grow in the Lord more and more of our life should reflect His. The appropriation of doctrines will become richer and richer as we see Him in the daily fellowship we have with Christ.

Transformation

Paul, while contrasting our spiritual growth in the New Testament to Old Testament events hit the Corinthians with a shocking truth in 2 Corinthians 3:18: But we all, with unveiled face, beholding as in a mirror the glory of the Lord, are being transformed into the same image from glory to glory, just as from the Lord, the Spirit. The Corinthians made mirrors, but their surface faded as the material oxidized. They knew that a mirror was an imperfect reflection. However, Paul hit them with the truth of their need to be beholding the Lord. As they beheld the Lord they would be transformed into the same glorious image of Jesus Christ.

Adam was in the image of God but corrupted it through the fall. We as saints are being transformed into the image of the incorruptible. The Holy Spirit is directing our steps and conforming our minds and we are being transformed as we dwell with the God of the universe.

Conformation

Romans 8:29 tells us that we are being conformed to the image of Christ (similar to being transformed). Transformation is the changing of appearance, conformation is the changing of behavior. Our old self was crucified with Christ (our position) and our sin nature is being put to death (Phil. 3:10) and being conformed to that death so that our new life may be reflected in our condition.

Imitators and Doers

Paul appeals to us in Ephesians 5:1 that we should be imitators of God. And again in 1 Corinthians 4:16 and 11:1 to be imitators of him as he imitates Christ. This concept of imitation comes with several things we should consider: imitation requires that we observe the original, we understand the patterns, and then we duplicate those things in our own thinking and behavior. Unlike a comedian who does impressions we see and do things deeply and with the work and empowering of the Holy Spirit.

Thinkers

In Romans 12:1–3 we find that Paul delves into thinking. First tells believers to be presenting their bodies as a holy and living sacrifice; this is similar to the idea of walking by the Spirit rather than the flesh from Galatians 5:16. Then, as the Holy Spirit impacts our life He impacts our thinking in verse 2 and we begin to prove out what God's will is because His thinking impacts our thinking. We evaluate what is true and then act on that truth by faith. Verse 3 then tells us that biblical thinking will lead to humility in our interactions with others. Philippians 4:8–9 tells us "Finally, brethren, whatever is true, whatever is honorable, whatever is right, whatever is pure, whatever is lovely, whatever is of good repute, if there is any excellence and if anything worthy of praise, dwell on these things. The things you have learned and received and heard and seen in me, practice these things, and the God of peace will be with you." Paul is telling his believing readers that their thoughts should be on these good things. Not that they're not thinking, but that they're intentionally thinking.

Co-Dwellers

As eternal spiritual beings we must remember that we were designed to be in fellowship with God forever. While we're on this earth we can walk with, be with, commune with, fellowship with, love with, pray with, and yes, dwell with God as we are in Christ. In 1 John 4:12 the apostle John tells us that if we are abiding in God His love will be reflected. Just as Christ prayed to the Father, that dwelling is a co-dwelling. We see one another in the eyes of our Father: not as perfect in condition, but as in perfect in Christ, seated in the heavenlies. We are all dwelling together spiritually; may our dwelling together physically be just as rich with God's love in us.

Abiding as a Lens for the Christian Life

It's worth noting that as we study the scriptures looking for things that are true for and of the believer we do so with the lens of abiding. We start statements of our walk with the idea of abiding like so: As an abiding believer, of course I would do this thing. And we know that as we dwell with Christ, we will do those things as He empowers us through His Holy Spirit. It's important to recognize that as we dwell, we will be growing spiritually, but that eternal perfection is not expected on this earth. We grow in our walk with the Lord progressively. One day in the future our position and condition will unify, but as we walk on this earth our lens is one of abiding, fellowship, and hope for the return of our Lord.

Isaiah 53

Foretelling the Substitutionary Death of the Messiah

By Dr. Bradley W. Maston

These 12 simple verses are among the most powerful words which pen ever put to paper. The Magna Carta would blush to be compared to this short chapter, the Code of Hammurabi could hardly be mentioned in the same breath, and the Declaration of Independence would fade from the page were its importance to be compared to these 12 lines of Hebrew text. This passage, written 600 years before Jesus walked the earth, is the single most collected, focused and proof-positive evidence of the need, mission, and purpose of the coming Messiah that can be found. To be quite clear, there are many other wonderful and clear passages of prophecy, to be sure, but in any list of messianic prophecies this passage will always rise to the top. We can be thankful for the variety of different pictures, types, and allusions to the Messiah that are revealed in the Old Testament. We can be thankful for the many other clear pictures and promises about Messiah's coming, but this passage is so central and so clear that no reader could ever dare to say that the interpreter is reading the Jesus story into this passage. This passage, when read honestly, simply gives a portrait of the ministry and purpose of Jesus Christ.

Furthermore, every Christian should be familiar with the inner workings of this precious passage of Scripture. We find that there are many wonderful accounts of the content of the gospel. But when it comes to the point, we must have passages like John 3:16, 1 Corinthians 15:1–5, and Romans 5:8 readily on our tongue so that we can follow Peter's admonition in 1 Peter 3:15:

> But sanctify the Lord God in your hearts, and always be ready to give a defense to everyone who asks you a reason

> for the hope that is in you, with meekness and fear…(NKJV)[1]

Yet in many ways Isaiah 53 shows its greatness among the fine company of passages that distill the message of the faith. It is a remarkable thing of Church history that there have been so many wonderful creeds to encapsulate the whole of the Christian faith to a greater or lesser degree. Yet this passage of God's holy word sees to do a much better job at characterizing the essentials of Christian doctrine, belief, and practice.

Isaiah 53 begins with what may almost seem a complaint. Isaiah lived his entire life as a recognized prophet of God. He stood before King Ahaz and King Hezekiah, and his prophetic utterances were well recognized as finding their source in God's revelatory power. Yet, even in this flood of wonderful news there was little audience for his reports. This finds its analogue in the time of Christ. While Jesus had a large following indeed, it was not a majority following among the nation of Israel. Jesus' following was even less than Isaiah's regarding the leadership of Israel. Among the Pharisees and the Sadducees alike there was very little support. To the point that the response of Nicodemus would be a noteworthy event in the gospel of John – because he was among very few who believed the report.

The next statement is written in the typical style of Hebrew poetry - rhyming themes and meanings, rather than mere phonetic patterns. The report of Isaiah had very specific content and it is described here as the revelation of the arm of the Lord. The phrase "the arm of the Lord" is a clear statement that Isaiah's message contains the very plan and power of God. As the Zondervan Illustrated Bible Dictionary writes about the arm in Biblical imagery:

> In the Bible, the upper human limb is often used as a figure for personal, active power. Thus the Lord lays "bare his holy arm" (Isa. 52:10), rather as we might say of someone about to undertake some task, "he rolled up his sleeves."

---

[1] Unless otherwise noted, all scripture quotations in this chapter are taken from the NKJV.

> The Lord's arm (53:1) is figuratively his personal intervention.[2]

This verse functions as a sort of headline of emphasis on the content which is to come. It is quite interesting that many of the Jewish Bible students of Christ's day would anticipate two Messiahs – one to suffer (*Ha Mashiach ben Joseph*) and one to reign (*Ha Mashiach ben David*). Even more remarkable was the belief of some that the relative obedience or disobedience of the Jewish people would determine which Messiah would be sent. Yet, here we see, in keeping with the rest of Scripture, that the Lord's first coming to earth was by no means optional. In fact, it was the greatest display of His very power and plan. The phrase "arm of the Lord" is used many other places in Scripture and time forbids evaluating each of them, so one example will suffice:

> **17** "If you should say in your heart, 'These nations are greater than I; how can I dispossess them?'— **18** you shall not be afraid of them, *but* you shall remember well what the Lord your God did to Pharaoh and to all Egypt: **19** the great trials which your eyes saw, the signs and the wonders, the mighty hand and the outstretched arm, by which the Lord your God brought you out. So shall the Lord your God do to all the peoples of whom you are afraid. (Deut. 7:17–19)

These verses equate the outstretched arm of the Lord has done. Included within this scripture is the entire set of world-changing plagues that the Lord poured out upon Egypt for His own glory. This was the central redemptive work of God described in the Torah, and it is rightly the most common reference point throughout the Tanakh for the power and faithfulness of God. Thus, this expression ("the arm of the Lord") is not a casual phrase, and it is vital to note that it is not used in Isaiah 53 to describe the triumphant second coming of the Messiah though it would be appropriate. Here it is used to describe the suffering of Messiah, for paying for and removing sin. This is, in

[2] Zondervan Illustrated Bible Dictionary, p. 118.

many ways, a far more adequate display of the power and character of God than was the amazing power which was shown at the Exodus.

This powerful prophetic poem continues in verse 2: "For He shall grow up before Him as a tender plant, and as a root out of dry ground." Here, more vital information about the Messiah pours forth. First, the Messiah would "grow up." He would not step onto the scene fully formed but would rather go through the steps of normal human birth, youth, adolescence, and adulthood. The next thing that is seen is that the Messiah would grow up "before Him."; the referent here clearly being God the Father. The picture here is of a dry and dead landscape devoid of the vital water needed for a garden to grow, yet bursting forth is this tender plant, a shoot or sapling out of the ground. The promise of life and great vulnerability is in view. The all-powerful, almighty, Godman, Messiah would be vulnerable. The image of a root coming forth from the dry ground also enforces the picture of the desperate need of man and the reality that the plan of God brings forth life, hope and the possibility for redemption.

Isaiah 53:2 continues by giving a rare and precious bit of information about the earthly body of the Savior. We are told that He has "no form or comeliness" and "no beauty". This is particularly looking at the outward traits of the Messiah. If men were to design their own Savior, we would make him the tallest, strongest, and most attractive human ever to walk this bare earth. We would design Him as one who would stand head and shoulders above all others in every single way. That, however, was not God's plan. The Messiah would not be marked by any earthly beauty, and He was not the type of person that would draw the eye while standing in a crowd or waiting in a line. Somehow, this vital detail is missed in nearly every picture or film version of the life of Christ. He is always rather attractive, handsome, tall, and shapely by our modern western standards. Yet, nothing could be further from the truth. When Christ came and identified with humanity it wasn't with the advantage of a remarkable form, or great physical charisma. He would have been normal, blandly unremarkable – in terms of His appearance – which tells us a great deal about His character and His mission. God *chose* for the Messiah to be common; it was an active work of the Will of God. Clearly, the divine input into the creation of the infant Messiah could have shaped his face and body to whatever shape was desirable. But God demanded that He be common, normal, average – because He was not coming to save the best and the brightest – he was coming to save all who would trust in Him.

Verse 3 describes the next major point of the Messiah's ministry. Rather than given the king's welcome He deserved, He would be rejected; not only rejected but openly despised and reviled. This is worth great note because humans tend to raise up those who demonstrate power. Those who are compassionate and powerful attract a very large audience. For examples of this we could look at the positive light in which Oprah, Bill Gates and others are often portrayed. They are very rich, but very generous with that wealth for the good of others. Yet neither Oprah nor Bill Gates have done anything to the measure of Jesus' life on earth. In His ministry, He cured incurable disease, saved hopeless demoniacs, controlled the elements themselves and called people back from the very grave. His power was clearly limitless and used for the benefit of others entirely. Yet, this remarkable prophecy is fulfilled in that the Messiah's earthly ministry was small in terms of followers. In fact, there were many who were ashamed of Jesus and would deny that they were with Him, as was evidenced by Peter, at the night of the crucifixion. Jesus was clearly despised by the world, but we did not know His worth. It would be difficult to imagine explaining to Pilate that his lack of moral fiber would cause Him to crucify the centerpiece of human history.

Humanities reaction and failure set the stage more fully for the statement of the Messiah's mission. While there are surely more passages about the Messiah's reign upon earth, there is no more important feature to His ministry than His sacrifice. It is amazing that it would take the Church until the St. Anselm in the 11th century before this very important doctrine of the substitutionary death of Christ would become plain to the church at large. Yet here the doctrine of substitution is strikingly plain. Messiah has the centrally important task of bearing something. The word "bear" translates the Hebrew word *nasa'* which means to bear up, pick up, or to take away. What He bore was the griefs of Israel and humanity. It is important to note that our griefs and sorrows are all the result of sin within the world. Israel's griefs existed almost entirely because of her own disobedience to God. Yet, all these griefs are said to be born up, taken away and carried off (*cabal* – to carry a great load or burden) all of humanities sorrows.

Moving back to the viewpoint of humanity, verse 4b foretells that there would not be recognition of what Christ accomplished on the part of his contemporaries. Quite to the contrary, the human accounting of the situation will be that the Lord Himself must have stricken and afflicted this Man. Even with this perfect preview in the prophetic word, it is the case that humanity missed the Messiah altogether, imagining that God himself was against Him. This is clear throughout the earthly life of Jesus, as the religious leaders, political leaders and demonic powers all set themselves together against Him as a united force. Again, this was never portrayed more clearly than at the cross of Jesus Christ.

Verse five continues to explain the nature of this substitutionary work of the Messiah. It must be noted how very insistent Isaiah is to make clear that "we" (humanity) brought the sin and failure; "He" the Messiah, bore the penalty in His flesh. We also see that that penalty clearly involved great physical agony and violence. The Messiah is said to be wounded for our transgressions, the word here having the very sense of a fatal and piercing wound – describing the crucifixion with remarkable accuracy. The bruising which fell upon Him was for the purpose of paying for our iniquities and failures. We see in very graphic and repeated terms the reality of what the Messiah would do and for what cause. It is only an exercise in imagination, but one must wonder if a ten-year-old Jesus of Nazareth read this passage and shuddered, if a tear came to His eye. We could only assume that glance at his family members, for whose transgressions He would die, would then steel His resolve to move forward in the plan of God.

The chastisement of our peace was laid upon Him. Because of His horrific ordeal the sin-torn soul of man could be made whole once more. The Hebrew word for peace (*shalom)* is far more thorough than a simple absence of conflict. The *shalom* which one Jew wishes another each morning is a fullness, wholeness, completeness that knows neither lack nor need. It was this peace which was wrought for humanity at the cross. It was the reality of sin which ruined the wholeness and peace of humanity and the earth. It was the payment of Jesus Christ which brings the only genuine offer of peace for humanity now. It was this peace that Jesus would promise to leave with us, and that He did not give as the world gives (Jn. 14:27).

We are told in verse 5 that it is by His very stripes that we are healed. This specific prophecy clearly was fulfilled by the multiple beatings of Jesus Christ. From Jewish flogging to Roman flogging the Messiah endured great physical pain in the course of His death. Pause must be taken to make a note of the incredible unlikeliness of this type of physical death afflicting any one person. One could, perhaps, predict that the Messiah would die terribly. After all, many good men have died terrible deaths throughout history. Yet, the specificity and brutality of the Messiah's death is laid out here with power and accuracy that could never be written except through divine revelation.

Verse 6 encapsulates the situation fully. Humanity is portrayed as a straying sheep. As a shepherd friend of mine once told me, sheep are pack animals, they only stray when something is seriously wrong with them. Such it is for lost humanity, each one strayed completely and fully from the clear path and way of God. We each find ourselves individually in this place of absolute need before the perfect provision of God. Having each gone down our own sorry path, we have found that each of our paths may be different, but they all end in the same place of death and despair. But it was the Lord's sovereign choice to lay the sins of all of us on the Messiah Jesus Christ. This passage of scripture is well attributed to its ancient author, Isaiah, but if we didn't know better, we may have thought this passage was written by Paul who wrote the following passages:

> But God demonstrates His own love toward us, in that while we were still sinners, Christ died for us. (Rom. 5:8)

> [3]For I delivered to you first of all that which I also received: that Christ died for our sins according to the Scriptures, [4]and that He was buried, and that He rose again the third day according to the Scriptures… (1 Cor. 15:3–4)

> This is a faithful saying and worthy of all acceptance, that Christ Jesus came into the world to save sinners, of whom I am chief. (1 Tim. 1:15)

It is an important point to keep in mind in today's world, which is rich with deception, regarding the teaching of the substitutionary death of the Messiah. This was by no means an innovation of Paul or the early church, but rather a teaching that came directly from the Old Testament as the only true hope for humanity.

Verse 7 gives prophetic reference to the conduct of Messiah as He endured His ordeal. There would be every opportunity for the Lord to flee, for the Lord to speak up. Each of the Lord's trials was illegitimate from every perspective, particularly from the classical Jewish perspective that would have forbid same day capital punishment trials, as well as trials by night. Yet, Christ never once raised His voice against the obscene mockery of justice that was taking place. Rather, He was silent before His murderers and allowed darkness to have its horrible hour.

The account continues and makes very clear in Isaiah 53:8 that Messiah had to die. The punishment and brutalization of the Godman would not be enough. He had to be physically killed and cut off from the land of the living. Again, the specific statements that imprisonment and trials (no matter how unlawful) would be a part of the Messianic death is another striking example of the accuracy of God's prophecy as put forth in the book of Isaiah. The punishment being pushed all the way to its conclusion of physical death the constant refrain of substitution is again sounded. This poetic work constantly repeats why this tragedy occurred – that sin had to be paid for, and Messiah alone could foot the bill. We can never think that the death of Christ was some sort of failure in the plan of God; rather it was the design of God from before the foundation of the world.

In the continuation of the prophetic message given to Isaiah, information about the Messiah's burial is revealed. A vagrant preacher would have very little opportunity to be well buried. A victim of a Roman crucifixion had only one destiny: the dead corpse would be flung in the communal valley burning trash. Yet, Jesus' body did not lie in the refuse. His body was claimed and laid in a newly cut tomb of a rich man (Mt. 27:60; Jn. 19:38). The sinless innocence of Messiah is here foretold as there would be no violence that anyone could lay to His account, and not one untruth that could be brought before Him. Verse 10 gives the motivation of the Lord as pleasure. The Lord took pleasure in this cruel destruction of the Messiah. The grief and pain of the Messiah was to the pleasure of God. The explanation of this unexpected reaction on the part of God the Father is forthcoming: The Father made the Son's soul an offering for sin. The Hebrew word translated "His soul" is the word *nephesh*, which can simply mean physical life, but generally has a sense of the immaterial part of man that gives himself consciousness. It is yet more evidence that the wholly divine Messiah would also have a wholly human soul.

Completing the Old Testament picture, the Messiah is called "an offering for sin." This completes the picture for the astute reader of the Torah. The idea of substitutionary, blood sacrifice began at the Garden of Eden, when God killed an animal to provide a covering for Adam and Eve. It continued though Cain and Abel when Cain's bloodless sacrifice was rejected. It reached a very high point indeed when Abraham was asked to offer up his own Son Isaac to the Lord, though the Lord stopped him – it would be much later that the Lord would provide the Lamb as Abraham promised. The blood sacrifice was again seen at the Passover, when the blood of a perfect lamb would be the sign that would cause the Spirit to pass over those houses bearing faithful Jews. The sacrificial system kept regular sacrifices for sin as well as the great annual observation of *Yom Kippur* and the beautiful substitutionary image of sin being placed upon an animal and sent away. These were mere shadows of this moment of which Isaiah writes so eloquently.

The final clear statement in this passage is the declaration of the resurrection. The Messiah would not remain dead, though He would absolutely die. He would prolong His days forth into eternity. He would look upon the labor of His soul and be satisfied. As we sit in this momentary interregnum between the two comings of Jesus Christ, it is certain that He sees the good work of His hand and how many He has justified thereby. We await the time when the Lord will assign Him His portion with the great. As the Psalms point out so beautifully:

> 6"Yet I have set My King On My holy hill of Zion." 7I will declare the decree: The LORD has said to Me, 'You are My Son, Today I have begotten You. 8Ask of Me, and I will give You The nations for Your inheritance, And the ends of the earth for Your possession. (Psa. 2:6–8)

> The LORD said to my Lord, "Sit at My right hand, Till I make Your enemies Your footstool." (Psa. 110:1)

Or as we, the Raptured Church, will one-day sing:

> [9]And they sang a new song, saying: "You are worthy to take the scroll, And to open its seals; For You were slain, And have redeemed us to God by Your blood Out of every tribe and tongue and people and nation, [10]And have made us kings and priests to our God; And we shall reign on the earth." (Rev. 5:9–10)

The 53rd chapter of the book of the Prophet Isaiah is beyond miraculous in its content. It gives clear and unquestionable information about the Messiah, and impossible to replicate demands for Messianic fulfillment. This passage leaves only one option in all human history as the resounding choice of God: Jesus of Nazareth is the Messiah. Perfect and holy, He is the chosen instrument of God by which men can be freed from Sin. He did this by His sacrificial, substitutionary death for all of humanity who would trust in Him for salvation. This remarkable passage certifies completely that Jesus Christ is the Messiah and gives the full significance of what He has done, and what He has yet to do!

THE SUFFICIENCY OF SCRIPTURE

The Believer's Sole Means of Growth and Fellowship with God

By Pastor Jacob Patrick Heaton

Introduction

The Bible is rightly held up to be the primary source of knowing and understanding the God who created heaven and earth, and the God who supplied the way of salvation through faith in Jesus' substitutionary death on the cross. Many Christians declare their belief in the sufficiency of Scripture without following their profession in their daily practice. If the Bible is sufficient, we as Christians should be careful when we come across secondary means that promise what only the Bible can give. In areas of Christian growth and enjoying fellowship with God, only the Bible can deliver an authoritative word. Only the 66 books of the Bible are worthwhile for a believer to develop towards maturity in Christ, and to enjoy intimacy with the God who is revealed in its pages.

Before we can draw proper conclusions about the Bible's sufficiency, the doctrine of the sufficiency of Scripture needs to be explained. There are three important points of contact to hit that deal with the doctrine of the sufficiency of Scripture. A student of this doctrine must define Scripture, sufficiency, and what it is that Scripture is sufficient to do. The next logical step is to hear the testimony of Scripture itself, in regard to what it is sufficient to do, and if anything else is permitted for growing a believer and cultivating fellowship with God.

THE DOCTRINE OF THE SUFFICIENCY OF SCRIPTURE

The first point is to settle the definition of the term "Scripture." Scripture is all that is God-breathed and produced by God in the moving of human authors to communicate His revealed truth (cf. 2

Tim. 3:16, 2 Pet. 1:20–21). It is the self-disclosure or revelation of God which has been defined as "the communicating to man what otherwise man would not know."[3] Scripture, therefore, is the holy writing that reveals God's authoritative truth to man. The revelation of God increases the understanding of man, but it doesn't level the playing field between God and man altogether. Paul Henebury remarks on this fact, "The doctrine of revelation does not promote autonomy but dependence on God; dependence on God not just for our everyday needs, but also for our everyday thinking."[4] Scripture is, and only will be, the compiled writings of the 66 books in the Bible. Since Scripture is God-breathed and carries the necessary authority that is due, it is the primary means by which mankind can understand the Creator of all things. Though it can be affirmed that Scripture is on the top shelf when it comes to revelation, it should be checked whether it is sufficient in supplying the necessary truth for the believer to grow and have fellowship with God. The obedient follower of Christ must determine whether Scripture is sufficient by itself, or if other means are necessary to walk as an obedient Christian.

The next important point of contact to handling the sufficiency of Scripture is to determine what the term sufficient means, and what the implications are for something being sufficient. Sufficient, according to Webster, means "as much as is needed."[5] Applying this definition of sufficiency to our discussion on the Scriptures, if Scripture is sufficient, then it is all that is needed. As important terms in the question on the sufficiency of Scripture are defined, the question remains, "what is Scripture sufficient in accomplishing?" What does Scripture say and do that leads one to accept that it is all that is needed? This question introduces a topic far too extensive to be adequately managed in this paper. The purpose and function of Scripture is the final point of contact that must be hit if any satisfactory grasp of the doctrine is to be achieved at all.

---

[3] Chafer, *Systematic Theology,* vol. 1, p. 48.

[4] Henebury "The Primacy of Revelation (part 1)".

[5] Webster, *Webster's Dictionary*, p. 644.

After defining what Scripture is, and what sufficiency entails, the next reasonable step is to ask, "sufficient for what?" If it is proposed that Scripture is sufficient, it must be determined to what extent its sufficiency reaches. If all three important points of contact are hit squarely, an adequate summary takes shape. The existence of Scripture declares that there exists a purpose and intention of God to reveal something.

There are eight considerations for arriving at a worthy conclusion to the purpose and function of Scripture. It has already been noted that revelation is making known what man by himself could not know about God. Therefore, the first point of consideration is that God purposed to make Himself known. There are different means by which God reveals Himself. Scripture is by far the most specific form of revelation. Therefore, in focusing on the written revelation, it is insightful to note that God used the language of man to reveal Himself. This insight is the second consideration, that the purpose of Scripture is to reveal to man certain truths about God intended to be understood. God created man with the ability to communicate and took steps to produce Scripture, then delivered it to man, proving that He intended His written revelation to be understood.

The last six considerations for the purpose and function of Scripture are revealed by looking at a key passage found in 2 Timothy 3:16–17.

> All Scripture is given by inspiration of God, and is profitable for doctrine, for reproof, for correction, for instruction in righteousness, that the man of God may be complete, thoroughly equipped for every good work.

The third consideration is that Scripture is profitable for doctrine. Other translations have "teaching." An important function of the Bible, according to this verse, is to teach certain truths about God. The fourth consideration is that Scripture is profitable for reproof. This declares the ability of Scripture to expose what is wrong in a person's life, and to bring upon that person a recognition of wrongdoing, or to identify a need for correction. A natural by-product of revealing what is wrong is the expectation that how to get right is included in the function of Scripture. The fifth consideration reveals the ability of Scripture to correct wrong thinking or behavior. It shows how to right the wrong. Specifically, Scripture contains the way to get right with God. The sixth consideration is that Scripture has the purpose and function of instructing in righteousness. Other Bible translations use the word "training." Training for righteousness carries the idea of working into permanent practice the things previously stated. Put another way; it teaches what is right, what is wrong, how to get right, and how to stay right.[6]

The seventh consideration is that Scripture functions to make a believer "complete" (lit. well fitted). Picture a man preparing for a dangerous journey but having everything he needs for achieving safe passage at his disposal.

The final consideration of the function and purpose of Scripture is to thoroughly equip the believer for every good work. This final consideration has two parts to it. The first part is that the believer needs nothing in addition to the Word of God to DO good works. The second part is the believer needs only Scripture to have every KIND of good work produced in their life. The considerations that come from 2 Timothy 3:16–17 are well summarized by Chuck Deveau, who says, "Nothing needs to be taught which it does not teach. Nothing needs to be censured, which it does not censure. Nothing needs correction that it does not correct. And no training need be given that it does not give.[7] To summarize all eight considerations above, Scripture is sufficient to grow a believer and to direct them into enjoying fellowship with God, their Creator.

Scripture is sufficient in the areas of growth in the Christian life, fellowship with God, and the achievement of safe passage through our earthly sojourn as Christians. An important question is raised by Edward Dingess, "if the word of God is deficient in any area, then to

---

[6] Wiersbe, *The Bible Exposition Commentary* vol. 2, p. 253.

[7] Deveau, *The Sufficiency of Scripture and God's Will*, 4.

what authority do we turn to place our trust in so that these areas of man's needs may be addressed?"[8]

However, Scripture is sufficient. It is truth revealed about God, from God, and is the making known to mankind what they would otherwise not know. Because of this, the revelation of Scripture carries the authority it is rightly owed. Scripture, therefore, is all that is needed to achieve safe passage through the dangerous world system that is headed up by the adversary, Satan. It is sufficient for the believer to give wisdom that counteracts the world's wisdom that is earthly, sensual, and demonic (Jas. 3:15). The purposes and functions of Scripture clearly show that nothing else is required to experience growth and to enjoy fellowship with God. However, this does leave the important question of whether additions to the Biblical text are permitted. Are there supplements that assist Scripture in the growth of a believer and their fellowship with God? Though nothing else is required, does this fact exclude any other means that might be used to cultivate growth?

Based on the function and purpose of Scripture laid out previously, and the reality that Scripture is all that is needed for a believer, it should be concluded that, if possible, supplements exist they should not be pursued. Supplements to aid the Scriptures' role in growing believers, and fellowship with God, are uncertain and unreliable sources. They do not follow the second consideration above, that God communicated to be understood. If something cannot be understood or understood with certainty, it should be handled with extreme caution, if handled at all. Therefore, supplements or practices outside of the Scriptures that promise growth or fellowship with God should not be searched out or heeded because the Word of God is all that is needed for growth and fellowship in the life of a believer. Unless of course, the supplement understands the proper authority of Scripture and seeks only to communicate the truths in Scripture or apply its principles.

---

[8] Edward A. Dingess, *The sufficiency of Scripture.*

THE TESTIMONY OF SCRIPTURE

The Scriptures have been proposed, thus far, to be sufficient in being the supreme means of truth, leading to the believer's growth and access to intimate fellowship with God. The God of the Bible is known through the study of the Bible. It is from the Bible alone the believer should look to receive the truth necessary for their walk as a Christian. Six passages in the Bible deliver powerful testimony to the Scriptures' ability and sufficiency in the life of a believer. Making some important observations from each of these passages will further defend the proper conclusion of the sufficiency of Scripture.

The first passage that testifies to the sufficiency of Scripture was dealt with in the earlier section and is found in 2 Timothy 3:16–17. It was shown that Scripture could teach, rebuke, correct, and train in righteousness. When rightly used, this ability results in a believer being thoroughly equipped for every good work. Because Scripture alone is mentioned in this passage as being what thoroughly equips the believer for every good work, it is necessary to conclude that nothing else is required. Therefore, regarding Christian living, no other source should be searched out or tolerated.

The second passage to look at has been said to be "the most comprehensive statement regarding the sufficiency of Scripture."[9] The passage is Psalm 19:7–14. In looking at this passage, several truths are packed into the short Psalm. In this Psalm written by David, seven truths should draw one's attention and testify to the ability of Scripture. The first truth is that the Word of God is perfect in its accuracy and strength, and it is converting (lit. restorative) to the soul of man. (v. 7) The second truth is that Scripture is "sure" (NKJV) and makes wise the simple. (v. 7) Scripture being sure has to do with the strength of the Word of God in relation to duration. Therefore, Scripture has a permanency to the truth it teaches, and the nature of its lessons are unfading. This is the reason for the simple being made wise. The third truth is that the Scriptures are right. (v. 8) In that, they are the full and complete truth. The Bible contains no errors and gives

---

[9] MacArthur, *The Sufficiency of Scripture*, 165.

a reason for the human heart to rejoice because of its testimony. The fourth truth is that Scripture is pure and enlightening to the eyes. (v. 8) The purity of the commands of God speaks to the intentions of God's Word to bring about purity. In other words, Scripture shows us how to be pure and is enlightening to the eyes that behold it. The fifth truth speaks to the production of the Word of God being the fear of the Lord that is clean and endures forever. (v. 9) The sixth truth is that the judgment of God's Word is true and righteous. (v. 9) The seventh truth is that the Word of God is more valuable than gold and sweeter than honey. This Psalm describes the qualities of the Word of God, and how they are the qualities befitting a life that is progressively maturing and enjoying a higher level of intimacy with God.

The third passage testifying to the sufficiency of Scripture is perhaps the most potent. 2 Peter 1:2–4 reveals five key observations. In Peter's introduction, he says that "grace and peace be multiplied to you in the knowledge of God and of Jesus our Lord." In other words, grace and peace are the abundant by-products of knowing God. Another potent observation is that the divine power has given "all things that pertain to life and godliness THROUGH THE KNOWLEDGE of Him" (emphasis my own). In no uncertain terms does Peter announce to his believing audience that anything needed in life and godly living comes from the knowledge of Jesus. The third observation reveals that this knowledge is most likely from the written word of God. Following a brief discourse on Christian virtues needing to be added to faith, Peter reveals his intentions of leaving a reminder after his death (cf. 2 Pet. 1:12–15). This reminder is most likely a reference to the written Word of God. The fourth observation helps to solidify this most likely conclusion. Peter begins talking about leaving a constant reminder of the truths that result in the multiplication of grace and peace and obtaining all things pertaining to life and godliness. In the context that follows this discussion of knowledge and Peter's intentions to leave behind a reminder after his death, an important passage is written, revealing key truth concerning the doctrine of inspiration. This knowledge that Peter will be "careful to ensure" is left as a reminder (v. 15) comes from him being an eyewitness of Jesus' earthly ministry, and more specifically, the transfiguration of Christ on the mount (2 Pet. 1:16–18). But his eyewitness alone is not the potency of this passage. The fifth key observation is seen in Peter, giving the source of Scripture. He says, "holy men of God spoke as they were moved by the Holy Spirit" (v. 21). In the contextual flow of thought that Peter is on, it is apparent that the knowledge of Jesus leading to all things pertaining to life and godliness are achieved by Scripture's revelation. Therefore, what we have in 2 Peter chapter 1 is a powerful testimony to the sufficiency of Scripture. If all things are supplied for the believer in the knowledge of Jesus from the Scriptures, there remains no room for supplementation to the life and godly living of the Christian. Scripture is sufficient.

The fourth passage testifying to the sufficiency of Scripture and its sufficiency for a believer's growth and fellowship with God is 1 John 1:1-4. John plainly states in 1 John 1:3 that "what was seen and heard was declared" to his audience, with the explicit purpose to bring about fellowship with the apostles and with God. We can observe that John's use of the word "us" in verses 1-3 is a reference to the apostles that were followers of Jesus while He was on the earth. John declares that what was from the beginning was something that "we have heard, which we have seen with our eyes, which we have looked upon, and our hands have handled." The only ones that the statement "from the beginning" would fit is the apostles (cf. Acts 1:21–22). The next important observation is that the phrase "word of life" appears to be connected to "the message" (v. 5). This would appear to be much more than just simply a reference to Jesus Himself but rather to what He taught about life. The message is said to be the reality of God being light and having no darkness in Him. Walking in the light or walking in the dark is contingent on whether the truth is practiced or not (cf. 1 Jn. 1:6). Therefore, the message being declared by John has to do with the teachings of Christ delivered to the apostles and passed on in the church age by those with apostolic authority (cf. Jn. 15:26–27, 16:12–13). As has already been mentioned, the things declared by John, which is the apostolic teaching for church age believers, was so "that you also may have fellowship with us; and truly our fellowship is with the Father and with His Son Jesus Christ." Therefore, the requirement for having fellowship with God is keeping with the teaching of the apostles. If anything else were needed for fellowship with God, this would be the place for John to mention it; however, he makes no mention of it. Scripture is sufficient.

The fifth passage gives strong testimony to the purpose and function of those who would handle the Word of God. Ephesians 4:11–15 reveals five different ministries of those who would handle the Word of God during the church age for the express purpose of edifying the body of Christ (v. 12). The duration of these ministries is until "we all come to the unity of the faith and of the knowledge of the Son of God" (v. 13). The first ministry listed is that of the apostles. apostles ministered in the first century and were eyewitnesses of the resurrected Christ. They were called by the Lord Jesus to reveal certain truths to the Church. The second ministry is that of the prophets. Prophets were individuals with the gift of revealing to man what man could otherwise not know. During the first century, apostles and prophets were used by God to communicate truth before the Church had a compiled list of inspired books that we now have in our 66 books of the Bible. Evangelists ministered in the early church, and this calling exists in modern times as well. The ministry of the evangelist has always been to proclaim the Gospel of Jesus Christ. Pastors were also given to the church with the purpose of edification. The pastor ministers as an under-shepherd to Jesus Christ and has the privilege of shepherding the flock of God. Their primary task is to feed the people of God with Biblical truth and to guard them against false teachers. The fifth ministry is that of a teacher. Teachers are men throughout Church history who have had the divine call to handle the Word of God, and to expose its message to the people of God.

These five ministries all have the same function, to edify the body of Christ. Furthermore, an additional observation in this text should be noted. Verse 14 explains the further purpose to these five ministries, and it is so that the people of God "should no longer be children, tossed to-and-fro and carried about with every wind of doctrine." This passage shows that the Word of God has two vital functions. The first function is to edify the body of Christ, to grow them until they reach full maturity. The second function is to guard against outward influences designed to trick and deceive the children of God.

The final passage is found in Hebrews 5:12–6:2, and it gives a lethal blow to those who would deny the doctrine of the sufficiency of Scripture. There are two crucial parts to this passage delivered to the first century Jewish Christian that was being tempted to go back to the passed away Judaic system of worship. The first part is that the writer of Hebrews delivers a rebuke to his audience concerning their lack of skill in the knowledge and use of God's Word. The first thing stated by the writer of Hebrews is "by this time you ought to be teachers" (5:12). There are two interesting facts contained in what is said. First, there is an expectation of progressive growth for believers. In the statement "by this time," it is revealed that these believers were in Christ for some time. This called for them to be further along in maturity than they were. Not only should these Christians have been further along, but the second interesting fact is that they should have been far enough along to be able to teach others the truths of God's Word. We observe that God's Word is the object spoken of in what the writer reveals next. He says, "you need someone to teach you again the first principles of the oracles of God" (5:12). The state of these believers was so inept that not only were they failing to teach, but they were deficient learners. They needed the "first principles of the oracles of God." They apparently needed to be retrained because their prior learning didn't take root in their life. The picture given is that these believers were like babies. The connection is that these believers were so unskilled in the Word of righteousness that they were like an infant unable to handle solid food. The intended image is that these believers were in serious spiritual crisis, being spiritually malnourished. The step needed to become an adult is to "by reason of use have their senses exercised to discern both good and evil" (5:14). The intended purpose of Scripture in this passage is that the word of God must be learned, used, exercised, and taught. The outcome of this progressive growth in the Word of God is the ability "to discern both good and evil" (5:14).

The second crucial part to understand in this passage is what role Scripture plays in the life of a believer. The writer of Hebrews draws a conclusion when he says "Therefore, leaving the discussion of the elementary principles of Christ, let us go on to perfection (lit. Maturity), not laying again the foundation" (6:1). The stated trajectory of the Christian life is to progress from the foundation of elementary truths, by putting them into practice in our lives. This step is followed by continuing in the path of learning Biblical truth and putting it into daily use, and consequently, growing in maturity as believers in Christ.

Because no additional sources for a believer's growth are mentioned in a passage dealing with a believer's growth, it must be concluded that any additions infringe upon the sufficiency of the Word of God. Much can be learned from Scripture when the student observes what is there. Additionally, a great deal can be learned when the student learns what isn't there, and as the proverbial saying goes, "the silence is deafening." Scripture is sufficient!

Conclusion

Scripture is the 66 books of the Bible and the written record to mankind, revealing the truth about God that man could not know if God did not reveal it. Because the testimony of Scripture soundly declares its sufficiency in matters relating to a believer's growth and fellowship with God, it is upheld that nothing else is needed. Though other things may promise growth or fellowship, there is no authority or way of knowing for sure whether those things are prescribed by God for growth or fellowship. Pastor Jeremy Thomas provides a concise summary of what is meant by the doctrine of the sufficiency of Scripture. He says, "they speak comprehensively to every area of life containing everything necessary for a life of godliness."[10] The comprehensiveness of Scripture should, therefore, exclude additional proposed means of growing as a Christian.

When a believer in Jesus Christ pursues additional sources outside of Scripture for knowing God and how to live before Him, they enter a minefield of potentially explosive false teaching set by the enemy, Satan. They are like a patient taking random medicine that a doctor would never prescribe, from people on the street. They are exposed to tremendous harm, damaging dependence, and reckless living. Only the

[10] Thomas, "Basics" Sermon Series.

Word of God is authoritative, and only the Scriptures are sufficient to set a child of God on the path of growth paved by God through what He has revealed.

This is not to say that books, classes, and various resources that address spiritual growth and maturity itself are restricted. Rather those books, classes and resources must share the self-declaring truth that Scripture alone is sufficient for growth. Therefore, those resources must direct the student to Scripture and not itself for the means of growth and maturity. Because Scripture is sufficient, and the supreme means by which the believer knows God.

BIBLIOGRAPHY

Chafer, Lewis S. *Systematic Theology: volumes 1 and 2.* Grand Rapids, MI: Kregel Publications, 1976.

Deveau, Chuck. "The Sufficiency of Scripture and God's Will 2 Timothy 3:13-17" *Chafer Theological Seminary Journal* 01:2. Summer, 1995.

Cone, Christopher. *Prolegomena on Biblical Hermeneutics and Method.* 2nd ed. Hurst, TX: Tyndale Seminary Press, 2012.

Dingess, Edward A. "The Sufficiency of Scripture" *Journal of Dispensational Theology* 10:30. September 2006.

MacArthur, John F. Jr. "The Sufficiency of Scripture" *Masters Seminary Journal* 15:2. Fall, 2004.

Henebury, Paul. "The primacy of Revelation (1)" *https://drreluctant.wordpress.com/ category/holy-Scripture/* (accessed April 27, 2019).

———. "The primacy of Revelation (2)" *https://drreluctant.wordpress.com/category/holy-Scripture/* (accessed April 27, 2019).

———. "The primacy of Revelation (3)" *https://drreluctant.wordpress.com/category/holy-Scripture/* (accessed April 27, 2019).

Thomas, Jeremy. *"Basics: Scripture."* Fredericksburg Bible Church, June 10, 2012. https://fbgbible.org/archive/B1223-061012.pdf

Wiersbe, Warren W. *The Bible Exposition Commentary*. Wheaton, IL: Victor Books, 1996.

CONSIDERING CALVINISM

By Ben Coleman

FOREWORD

My first exposure to the Calvinism conversation came when I was on a high school trip with a close friend and discovered that he doesn't believe God loves everyone. This was rather shocking to me at the time because I'd never heard that idea, especially not from a fellow believer I respected. That revelation immediately led to a lengthy conversation that went on and off throughout the rest of the day about how my friend had gotten to that point and all the other beliefs that came with it. We even stayed up until 2 AM that night talking. In the few weeks that followed that trip it seemed like all we really talked about was Calvinism.

Saying that we "talked" is putting it somewhat lightly. In ways we'd never experienced before when discussing our faith, my friend and I argued over these doctrines as to what the truth really was. We exchanged verses for hours but never seemed to really get anywhere; at the time neither of us had yet developed the important principles of Bible interpretation necessary to understand passages in their context and were rather flippant with our "proof-texts." As soon as I'd gotten home from the trip I set out to study and seek to understand Calvinism deeper, though primarily for the purpose of being able to persuade my friend more convincingly. As you might imagine, this was ultimately fruitless. Our arguments and even debate over these issues did nothing but create tension between us; we eventually decided not to talk about it anymore.

As I look back on all those conversations, I regret the way I handled them and the attitude both my friend and I demonstrated. Beyond being at least mildly abrasive, we really weren't listening to each other with any sort of humility or willingness to consider the potential that what the other person was saying was true. We so quickly hardened ourselves in our positions that neither of us were going to budge. What I regret in this is not that no one changed their mind, for there can be fruitful conversations that don't have that result. Instead, I regret that the pride we had in our position was more important to us than humbly seeking the truth; that being right was more important than a friend.

After those initial months of considering Calvinism my friend and I dropped the topic, and it remained off the table for us from then on. Even in my years at Bible college, where talking theology was a daily occurrence, doctrines like election and the hardening of God remained mostly out of the picture. Though I was growing in my ability to study the Bible, I never ventured back into Calvinism territory. In fact, during that time I became increasingly aware of the complexities involved in those types of doctrinal considerations and my position softened. I shifted more toward a neutral stance, perpetually confused as to why these were such controversial and dividing issues but yielding in my inability to discern the truth.

These doctrines bear great implications. What you believe about election, free-will, and the like makes a significant difference in your interpretation, your theology, and your actions. While there is a point at which further "beating a dead horse" isn't wise, it is regrettable to me that believers would avoid discussing such important topics. Hopefully, in a Christlike way, we can discuss even things we disagree on with the common purpose of coming to the most reasonable conclusions regarding the intended meaning of the biblical authors.

As it turned out, it was conversation with another great friend several years after Bible college that led to my return to considering these topics. Just as in the conversations with my high school friend, our starting points differed. Only this time, the conversation progressed with much more tact and depth. We'd both determined to give an honest and introspective evaluation of ourselves and the doctrines at hand. My genuine belief is that we were both more interested in mutual edification around pursuing the truth than in winning arguments. Because of that, the conversations were deeply enriching for both of us.

As you read this, please engage with the material as though you'd been along for those conversations, similarly interested in the truth. Know that my heart in this is to share the fruit of a great deal of research and point others to the truth as much as possible. While truth is by nature exclusive and explaining what I believe is true requires denying other positions, it is the positions I deny and not the people who hold them. I certainly mean no disrespect to those who disagree with me, and my sincerest hope is that the truth will ultimately prevail!

Before we begin, it would be helpful for us to get on the same page regarding what elements of Calvinism as a system this essay will focus on. While there certainly is a great deal that could be covered, we'll home in on what I deem to be the heart of the matter, which is twofold: whether God has already provided the potential for everyone to believe in Him (insinuating that people may freely choose Him) or has yet to provide that potential, and whether God determines individuals' salvation or they do. Explain what you believe about that, and you're already well on your way to defining what you believe about election, free-will, God's prevenient grace, and more. In fact, the Calvinist answers to those questions form the core ideas of the system that 1) no individual would ever choose to believe in Jesus, if they had the choice, and that 2) God is the one who determines salvation. Before we move forward, allow me to explain and illustrate.

Also, to aid your ability to understand me, know that when the words "determine" and "free will" are used throughout this essay, I mean the following:

- Determine – make a decision that will be actual (which of course requires the ability to actualize that choice) because no outside party will overturn it.
- Free will – the ability to choose among potential (capable of development into actuality) options while independent of coercive control.
- Note: influence does not constitute coercion because, by definition, a person is still capable of their own determination, regardless of what might be apparent.

INTRODUCTION

Mention the words election, predestination, and free-will in a Christian setting and you're quite likely to stir up quite a fuss. In fact, there have been a plethora of respected theologians who have disagreed with one another on these topics for centuries. Unfortunately, these tend to be polarizing issues which can lead even fellow believers who typically agree to be somewhat hostile toward one another.

Why hasn't a particular view prevailed as true? At least part of the answer to that question goes back to the fundamentals of how we study the Bible. When we approach a passage to determine its meaning, we apply the following process:

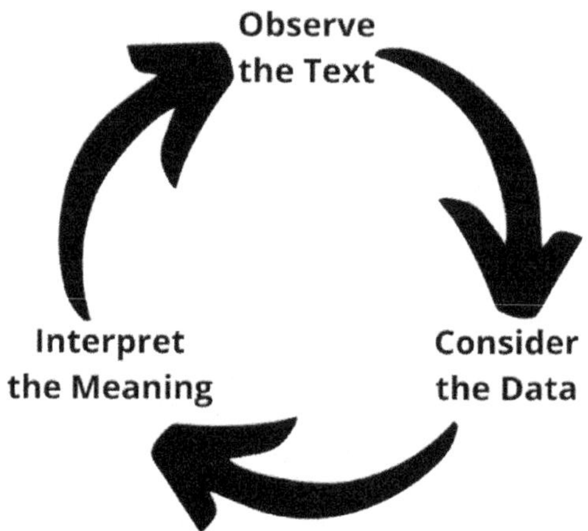

Ensuring that we accurately understand what the author meant is not always as simple as just reading the text; especially when separated by things like timing and cultural and language differences. Instead, we apply principles of interpretation to determine which data to rely on and how to weigh it all in our search for the most likely meaning. While this is a necessary and worthwhile process, the danger is that we can't avoid leaving room for our own presuppositions and bias to potentially impact our interpretation. If I have presupposed a certain meaning, then I'll be more likely to side with the data which supports it. This doesn't necessarily mean that my conclusion isn't the one the author wanted me to come to, but it does mean that my conclusion was driven at least partially by my own ideas rather than the text itself. In fact, the more we presuppose, the less we let the text speak for itself. We can't, however, just abandon presuppositions altogether. We couldn't function without some background from which to approach the world; and the same is true of God's Word. Every one of us has a framework for how we collectively understand what the Bible teaches and what is true, which we apply continuously.

Complicating the development of our Biblical frameworks, interpretations in one instance become presuppositions in another. As an example, believing that God is holy and righteous, without even the capability of committing sin, and then reading about Jesus becoming angry, would lead me to conclude that Jesus' anger was not sinful. This is a rather simple, over-the-plate example, but this was only one instance where a belief impacted the interpretation of another. When you consider all the correlation that goes on in Bible study, the web of passages offering interpretive guidance for one another compounds significantly and it becomes vital to carefully sift how presuppositions weigh in.

When it comes to topics like election and free will, we face a special challenge. Lacking explicit Biblical definitions and explanations, we put our framework to the task of reading between the lines. This is where presuppositions thrive. When we face passages that are less clear for us, it is all too easy to virtually pick what we'll believe they mean based on what best aligns with what we already believe. This is known as confirmation bias. We're less likely to change our mind about what we believe, even if doing so would result in us aligning with the truth, than we are to confirm what we already believe, even if driven primarily by faulty presuppositions. If we have an inkling as to what we think the truth is, we'll be more likely to favor the evidence for that understanding. By default, that position strengthens, which in turn fortifies presuppositions brought to future considerations. In this way building a framework is cyclical.

The reason that becomes problematic in this context is that it is difficult to dissect cyclical processes. Evaluating how a system's interpretations fit with the Biblical authors' intended meaning is virtually inconclusive because the interpretations are, by nature, a claim as to the meaning of the text. Everyone can claim their view is biblical because it represents what they believe the Bible means. Unfortunately, even examining verses individually is ineffective at providing an objective critique of a system because correlation is a necessary (and rightly so) element in Bible study. If I already believe, for instance, that propositions of system A are true, then I'll interpret individual verses in light of that. For that reason, it is especially important that we ask ourselves not only why we believe what we believe, but also what we want to believe, and whether that inkling is clouding objective evaluation of Biblical data.

Instead of "proof-texting," which we've already established holds little weight against presuppositions, this essay unwinds the cycle of Calvinist interpretation to look at its origin. As it turns out, history provides significant evidence for the idea that the system of Calvinism was generated out of attempts to syncretize God's Word with certain deterministic pagan philosophies. After examining this evidence, albeit quickly, we turn to consider several passages most central to the conversation. Lastly, given that Calvinism is philosophical in nature as well as theological, we'll analyze the reasoning involved.

CALVINISM'S AUGUSTINIAN ORIGIN

Pagan Philosophies During the Early Church

Stoicism, Neoplatonism, Gnosticism (particularly as it led to the following), and Manichaeism were schools of philosophy that were around and thriving during the days of the early Christian church. While they considered biblical ideas in constructing their belief systems, they favored reason over the Bible. Interestingly, these philosophical systems dealt with concepts such as the will of man, his responsibility toward God, God's justice, and more.

Stoicism taught that "every miniscule event in the universe was controlled by fate..." Even the famous Stoic Chrysopsis (ca. 279 – ca. 206 BCE) could not sidestep the implication that no one was ever capable of doing something they weren't determined to. Neoplatonism was "instituted by Plotinus (ca. 250) and popularized by Porphyry (ca.350)." The philosophy borrowed from Stoicism, teaching that "free choice must be restored by a divine infusion to restore the will" (see *Enneads* 3.2.9.1, 2.3.1.1, 3.3.19-21; 4.8.5.1). In the Neoplatonist view, man's decision to become physical, which combined soul with matter, introduced evil and represented the destruction of free choice. Gnosticism also taught that physical matter itself was evil and spiritual was good, which led to unbiblical conclusions regarding sin and Jesus Christ. They accepted the teaching that people are "hopelessly damned from birth" and that for anyone to be saved "the Gnostic god unilaterally restored right reason to the helplessly corrupted human will through a gift to the mind" (see *Corpus Hermeticum* 4.4; 6, 68.36; 6, 69.31–32 and Definitions of Hermes Trismegistus to Asclepius 5.3). The false prophet Mani, the father of Manichaeism, created his own sort of Gnosticism but with the goal of making it "a syncretistic (a combined) religion for all persons worldwide..." In his philosophy, "the 'enslaved will' cannot choose. it is damned until unilaterally released by 'reconciliation to God through Christ.'"

The Early Church and Augustine

The early church opposed these pagan philosophies and unanimously held the belief that individuals were free to determine their own response to the Gospel. Dr. Ken Wilson, in preparation for writing his doctoral dissertation at the University of Oxford, studied the works of eighty-four early (before AD 430) church fathers and found that over fifty of them addressed topics such as free will and God's foreknowledge, all of whom opposed the idea of divine determinism (God determining who is saved). For instance, Irenaeus of Lyons (ca. 180) vigorously opposed both Gnostic and the similar Stoic determinism (see *Adversus Haeresis* 1.6.2; 2.29.1–31; 2.14.4). Origen (ca. 185–254) argued extensively for the contrary idea that man is free in the choice of belief in Jesus in his third book of *De principiis* (see *Peri Archon* 3.1.6). Even Ambrose of Milan (d.397), who baptized Augustine, emphasized that man is capable of faith and that election depends on faith, rather than vice versa.

Interestingly, Saint Augustine of Hippo had been significantly involved in several of these philosophical systems prior to his conversion. He "spent ten years as a Manichean…", "was trained in Stoicism" to the point he "embraced it even after becoming a Christian," and even "credits his own conversion to Christianity as occurring through the philosophy of Neoplatonism" (see *Confessions* 7:9-16). Nevertheless, when he became a believer, he "gradually moved away from Neoplatonic and Manichaean ideas to embrace the Christian theology of his time." Despite his prior bent toward determinism, the converted Augustine proclaimed that "by his free will man has a means to believe in the Liberator and to receive grace" and "Nor did God predestine anyone except him whom He knew would believe and would follow the call, whom he [Paul] calls 'the elect'" (see *Exposition on Questions in the Epistle to the Romans*, 44.3 and 55, respectively). Even as late as when he became co-bishop of Hippo, he was still opposing the theology of the Manichaeans.

The Origin of Augustinian-Calvinism

Around A.D. 410, after Rome had been sacked by the Vandals, men named Pelagius and Caelestius came to Tunisia, where Augustine was at the time, and instigated what's now known as the "Pelagian Controversy." They were teaching heresies, including the idea that Adam's sin was a merely personal failure, and each subsequent human is born in the same state of creature innocence (not possessing a sin nature) that Adam had been in prior to the fall. In seeking to oppose proponents of these views, Augustine reconsidered his theological system; particularly the implications of salvation by infant baptism (which he believed). He reasoned that "1) The church baptizes infants, 2) Water baptism is for forgiveness of sin and reception of the Holy Spirit, 3) Some dying infants are rushed by their Christian parents to the bishop for baptism but die before this can occur, while other infants born of prostitutes are abandoned on the streets when a church virgin rushes them to the bishop who baptizes them, 4) These infants have no control over whether or not they are baptized and receive the Holy Spirit to become Christians, 5) Therefore, God must unilaterally and unconditionally predetermine which infants are damned and which are justified…" His key deduction was that, because infants didn't have personal sin, the forgiveness of sin given by infant baptism must have been to appease a guilt they'd inherited by Adam's first sin. In the course of such considerations, he revisited and reaffirmed some of his priorly held philosophies, relying on them in seeking to maintain logical consistency. The same logic was then extrapolated to the context of adults, and the system of Calvinism as we know it was born; though, of course, it wasn't called Calvinism until later (Augustine preceded the namesake of the system, John Calvin).

"Augustine used Christian Scriptures to prove his new doctrines. But unfortunately, he used Manichaean interpretations- the very interpretations he had previously refuted as heretical after becoming a Christian." His self-admitted proof-texts became Romans 5:12 and Proverbs 8:35. Later, he also reinterpreted passages such as Romans 7, 9, and 1 Corinthians 15 in trying to garnish biblical support. The bishop of Hippo openly admitted to having abandoned the long-held doctrine of human free choice in favor of the deliberately syncretistic philosophies of Manichaeism. He even went so far as to revise some of his prior writings, which opposed determinism, in favor of what he had come to believe.

The fact that Augustine even became a bishop, as an ex-Manichaean, was against the typical practice of church leadership. When he began reaffirming such philosophies from that position, then, other bishops vehemently opposed him. In fact, many leaders continued to reject divine determinism, down to the last Greek church father, John of Damascus. Of course, not everyone rejected his ideas. John Calvin, the namesake of the system, was deeply influenced by Augustine. In his *A Treatise on the Eternal Predestination of God*, Calvin acknowledged "Augustine is so wholly within me that I could write my entire theology out of his writings." Interestingly, Calvin had also been steeped in Stoicism. Later in history, reformer Martin Luther, an Augustinian monk, revived Augustine's deterministic theology, paving the way for the continuance of Calvinism as a strand of Reformed Theology.

So, you see, historical evidence points rather strongly to the idea that Augustine came to interpretations like these to back up the line of reasoning he was following, rather than coming to the logical system he did based solely on exegesis. This means Calvinism originated through the syncretism (attempt to harmonize) of pagan philosophy with the Bible. While this doesn't mean we can automatically reject his interpretations, it warrants caution and consideration as to how reasonable it is that sound exegetical study–and study that was unfamiliar with Calvinist presuppositions–would lead to the same conclusions.

BIBLICAL CONSIDERATION OF CALVINISM

Let's now consider the verses which seemingly support most strongly the Calvinist ideas that man, if given determination, would never believe in Jesus and that God determines who is saved. For the former, we'll examine John 6:44, Romans 3:10–12, and 1 Corinthians 2:14 in their context. For the latter, we'll examine Ephesians 1:4 and Romans 8:29–30 in their context. Our goal is to observe the biblical data and evaluate how deeply Calvinist interpretations are rooted in the context they're found in. Theoretically, if Augustine came to interpretations like these driven primarily by presuppositions and syncretism rather than sound exegesis, there may be traces of relative shallowness where the width of evidence contradicts the system.

John 6:35–40, 44–47, *and* 64–65

> Jesus said to them, "I am the bread of life; whoever comes
> to me shall not hunger, and whoever believes in me shall
> never thirst. 36 But I said to you that you have seen me and
> yet do not believe. 37 All that the Father gives me will come
> to me, and whoever comes to me I will never cast out. 38
> For I have come down from heaven, not to do my own will
> but the will of him who sent me. 39 And this is the will of

> him who sent me, that I should lose nothing of all that he has given me, but raise it up on the last day. [40] For this is the will of my Father, that everyone who looks on the Son and believes in him should have eternal life, and I will raise him up on the last day…" [44] No one can come to me unless the Father who sent me draws him. And I will raise him up on the last day. It is written in the Prophets, 'And they will all be taught by God.' Everyone who has heard and learned from the Father comes to me— [46] not that anyone has seen the Father except he who is from God; he has seen the Father. [47] Truly, truly, I say to you, whoever believes has eternal life… [64] But there are some of you who do not believe." (For Jesus knew from the beginning who those were who did not believe, and who it was who would betray him.) [65] And he said, "This is why I told you that no one can come to me unless it is granted him by the Father."

The Calvinist interpretation of the passage centers on verses 44, "No one can come to me unless the Father who sent me draws Him…" and 65, "...no one can come to me unless it is granted him by the Father," and claims that Jesus was teaching that no human being would respond by believing in Jesus if given the choice, but instead the only way for anyone to be saved is for God to determine they would be, which is irresistible. A famous proponent of Calvinism put it this way, "God's drawing is decisive; and without it, no one would come… the reasonings of fallen human beings are never the decisive reason anyone comes to [Jesus]. The decisive reason anyone comes to [Jesus] is that [the] Father draws Him." When we observe the context, it becomes clear that Jesus (as recorded by John) was most likely not seeking to teach a universal soteriological principle that no one can believe in Him unless God determines it. Instead, He was seeking to simultaneously hide the truth from the particular Jews questioning Him (John 6:60, 66) and explain why some of the Jews couldn't come to Him but others, like the disciples, could. He wasn't teaching universal soteriology, distinguishing the elect from unbelievers, but was speaking in a specific and unique context, distinguishing people of His day.

God purposed to reveal Himself in special ways to His disciples/apostles.

> And he answered them, 'To you it has been given to know the secrets of the kingdom of heaven.' (Mt. 13:11a)

> ...privately to His own disciples He explained everything." (Mk. 4:34b)

Scripture also teaches that these certain people were chosen for these roles based on God's plan.

> God raised Him up on the third day and granted that He be revealed, 41 not to all the people, but to witnesses who had been chosen beforehand by God, that is, to us who ate and drank with Him after He arose from the dead. (Acts 10:40–41)

> "I have revealed Your name to the men whom You gave Me out of the world; they were Yours and You gave them to Me, and they have followed Your word. [7] Now they have come to know that everything which You have given Me is from You; [8] for the words which You gave Me I have given to them; and they received them and truly understood that I came forth from You, and they believed that You sent Me... [11] Holy Father, keep them in your name, which you have given me, that they may be one, even as we are one. [12] While I was with them, I was keeping them in Your name, which You have given Me; and I guarded them, and not one of them perished except the son of destruction, so that the Scripture would be fulfilled. (Jn. 17:6–8, 11–12)

The Scripture in fulfillment here is Psalm 41:9, which John also refers to in John 13:18, both of which concern prophecy concerning Judas.

> Jesus answered, "I told you that I am he. So, if you seek me, let these men go." [9] This was to fulfill the word that he

> had spoken: "Of those whom you gave me I have lost not one." (Jn. 18:8–9)

These passages teach that God gave certain people to Jesus for Him to pour into, because they would eventually become apostles ("sent ones") with a special mission in the redemptive plan of God. We can't assume that this choice was God's determination of their salvation, however, because Judas was included with the chosen and was not saved.

> And when day came, he called his disciples and chose from them twelve, whom he named apostles. (Lk. 6:13)

> Jesus answered them, "Did I not choose you, the twelve? And yet one of you is a devil." (Jn. 6:70)

> Then after he [Judas, the son of Simon Iscariot, v. 26] had taken the morsel, Satan entered into him. (Jn. 13:27)

There were also many who believed in Jesus besides those that Scripture distinguishes as those who were given to Him.

> "I have revealed Your name to the men whom You gave Me out of the world… [20] I am not asking on behalf of these alone, but also for those who believe in Me through their word." (Jn. 17:6a, 20)

Those who were given to Jesus were a specific group of people, and that group is not all of the elect throughout time. John 6 contrasts those who were with Jesus from others in Israel at the time. Prior to the conversation in this passage, Jesus had fed the 5,000. The people who had come to talk to Him now sought Him "because [they] ate [their] fill of loaves" (v. 26). They asked Him what they must do "to be doing the works of God" (v. 28) and He told them that "you believe in Him whom He has sent" (v. 29). Immediately they asked Him for a sign so that they "may see and believe you?" The people wanted signs and wonders but weren't willing to accept the person of Jesus.

> So Jesus said to the Jews who had believed him, "If you abide in my word, you are truly my disciples, 32 and you will know the truth, and the truth will set you free." 33 They answered him, "We are offspring of Abraham and have never been enslaved to anyone. How is it that you say, 'You will become free'?" 34 Jesus answered them, "Truly, truly, I say to you, everyone who practices sin is a slave to sin. 35 The slave does not remain in the house forever; the son remains forever." (Jn. 8:31–35)

> Though he had done so many signs before them, they still did not believe in him… (Jn. 12:37)

Israel, at the time of Christ, pursued the law as if it were based on works (Rom. 9:31–32), sought to replace God's righteousness with their own (Rom. 10:3), and were a disobedient and contrary people (Rom. 10:21) that angered/grieved Jesus at their hardness of heart (Mark 3:7). He had performed many miracles before them and quite significantly revealed Himself to them, and yet they still wouldn't believe in Him. Jesus even said that some cities which had been most known for their wickedness would have changed their minds concerning Him if that amount of revelation had been given to them.

> Then he began to denounce the cities where most of his mighty works had been done, because they did not repent. 21 "Woe to you, Chorazin! Woe to you, Bethsaida! For if the mighty works done in you had been done in Tyre and Sidon, they would have repented long ago in sackcloth and ashes. 22 But I tell you, it will be more bearable on the day of judgment for Tyre and Sidon than for you. 23 And you, Capernaum, will you be exalted to heaven? You will be brought down to Hades. For if the mighty works done in you had been done in Sodom, it would have remained until this day. 24 But I tell you that it will be more tolerable on the day of judgment for the land of Sodom than for you." (Mt. 11:20-24)

Jesus is the only means of relationship with the Father (Jn. 14:6, 9). If a person rejects Jesus, they cannot have the Father.

> "If you had known me, you would have known my Father also. From now on you do know him and have seen him...
> 11 Believe me that I am in the Father and the Father is in me, or else believe on account of the works themselves." (Jn. 14:7, 11)

Of the group of Jews who had gone to speak with Jesus and seek more food, it was said "you do not have His word abiding in you, for you do not believe the one whom he has sent" (5:38). In 6:36 He told them "You have seen me and yet do not believe." In chapter 5 He said "For if you believed Moses, you would believe me; for he wrote of me.
47 But if you do not believe his writings, how will you believe my words?" (5:46–47). In other words, these Jews had the Word of God, but did not believe it, so of course they would not believe Jesus. In fact, earlier in chapter 5, Jesus had said "You search the Scriptures because you think that in them you have eternal life; and it is they that bear witness about me, 40 yet you refuse to come to me that you may have life" (5:39–40). These Jews did not believe God's Word and refused to come to Him (Jn. 1:11). In fact, Israel in general (though of course not every individual) had hardened their hearts toward Him and became calloused to the point they would not believe in Jesus.

> He came to his own, and his own people did not receive him. But as many as received Him, to them He gave the right to become children of God, to those who believe in His name. (Jn. 1:12)

Because of Israel's unbelief, impenitence, and rejection of God, He judicially hardened them by blinding their eyes, giving them a spirit of stupor, (Jesus) telling people to be silent about who He was, and speaking in parables. He even avoided those who sought to make Him king. This was how God hid further revelation of Jesus from those who had rejected Him and ensured that His purposes (particularly the crucifixion) at that point would be fulfilled.

> "But we impart a secret and hidden wisdom of God, which God decreed before the ages for our glory. [8] None of the rulers of this age understood this, for if they had, they would not have crucified the Lord of glory." (1 Cor. 2:7–8)

> "...this Jesus, delivered up according to the definite plan and foreknowledge of God, you crucified and killed by the hands of lawless men." (Acts 2:23)

> ...the rest were hardened; [8] just as it is written: "God gave them a spirit of stupor, eyes to see not and ears to hear not, down to this very day." (Rom. 11:7b-8)

> And as they were coming down the mountain, he charged them to tell no one what they had seen, until the Son of Man had risen from the dead. (Mk. 9:9)

> "This is why I speak to them in parables, because seeing they do not see, and hearing they do not hear, nor do they understand. [14] Indeed, in their case the prophecy of Isaiah is fulfilled that says: 'You will indeed hear but never understand, and you will indeed see but never perceive.' [15] For this people's heart has grown dull, and with their ears they can barely hear, and their eyes they have closed, lest they should see with their eyes and hear with their ears and understand with their heart and turn, and I would heal them." (Mt. 13:13–15)

> When the people saw the sign that he had done, they said, "This is indeed the Prophet who is to come into the world!" [15] Perceiving then that they were about to come and take him by force to make him king, Jesus withdrew again to the mountain by himself." (Jn. 6:14–15)

This judicial hardening and concealment of revelation was not God's determination that the people wouldn't believe in Jesus (Jn. 6:35, 47). Instead, the hardening was the only way for God to honor their own determination and see His plan (the crucifixion; 1 Cor. 2:7–8) completed.

> Though he had done so many signs before them, they still did not believe in him, [38] so that the word spoken by the prophet Isaiah might be fulfilled: "Lord, who has believed what he heard from us, and to whom has the arm of the Lord been revealed?" [39] Therefore they could not believe. For again Isaiah said, [40] "He has blinded their eyes and hardened their heart, lest they see with their eyes, and understand with their heart, and turn, and I would heal them."" (Jn. 12:37–40)

Bringing discussion back to the interpretation of John 6, we see that this is the passage in which Jesus explains why some had come to Jesus and others hadn't (indeed, couldn't). Jesus' own commentary on why He told them, "No one can come to me unless it is granted him by the Father" is, according to verses 64 and 65, that "there are some of you who do believe." Sure enough, in response to what Jesus said here, "many of His disciples turned back and no longer walked with Him" (6:66). Following that, Jesus wondered aloud whether His own disciples, too, would leave Him. Peter responded, "Lord, to whom shall we go? You have the words of eternal life, [69] and we have believed, and have come to know, that you are the Holy One of God" (6:68b–69). The twelve had believed in Jesus and come to know Him as the Messiah. Jesus responded, effectively concluding His teaching, "Did I not choose you, the twelve? And yet one of you is a devil" (6:70).

The Calvinist idea that, left to his own determination, man would never choose God and/or that the only way for someone to be saved is for God to determine that they believe is not a clear derivation from the passage. Arriving at that conclusion requires equating the word "come" with "believe," and determining that "draws," in the salvific sense, is only applicable to the elect (in fact, it's the causal factor in who will be saved). The meaning of these words, however, is nowhere necessitated to be thus in the grammar (Greek). The "him" after "draws" is not necessarily equating those drawn with those who will be raised up. The grammar is similar to the sentence "No one can join the Army unless they've been recruited, and those who've been recruited will be trained." We wouldn't take that to mean that the Army only intended to recruit those who are eventually trained, for clearly, they seek to recruit a lot of people who don't end up joining. The most reasonable understanding of the meaning of these verses, then, rests primarily on the context, which we've seen favors the interpretation that Jesus was distinguishing His disciples from the Jews who'd rejected Him. He was not teaching that the mechanism by which a person is saved is God's determination. He does, however, make a clear statement that salvation comes when a person believes. John 6:47, "Truly, truly, I say to you, he who believes has eternal life."

Romans 3:10–12

> …as it is written: "There is no righteous person, not even one; 11 There is no one who understands, There is no one who seeks out God; 12 They have all turned aside, together they have become corrupt; There is no one who does good, There is not even one."

This was originally recorded in Psalm 14:1–3, which says "The fool has said in his heart, 'There is no God.' They are corrupt, they have committed detestable acts; There is no one who does good. 2 The Lord has looked down from heaven upon the sons of mankind To see if there are any who understand, Who seek God. 3 They have all turned aside, together they are corrupt; There is no one who does good, not even one" and Psalm 53:1–3, which is almost identical to Psalm 14:1–3. The Calvinist understands the passage, based primarily on the phrase "there is no one who seeks out God," to teach that no individual would ever choose to believe in Jesus if they had the determination. I would put forth, however, for your consideration, the interpretation that Paul's primary emphasis was in relation to man's inability to be justified by the law, rather than man's inability to believe in Jesus.

In the context surrounding Romans 3, Paul's argument was that "by works of the law no human being will be justified in his sight" (Rom. 3:20a) because "both Jews and Greeks are under sin" (Rom. 3:9b) and "through the law comes knowledge of sin" (Rom. 3:20b). Citing that "There is no righteous person" and that "There is no one who seeks out God" supports Paul's claim that both Jews and Greeks were under sin. However, then Paul asserts that "But now the righteousness of God has been manifested apart from the law" (Rom. 3:21a). If not by the law, how does the righteousness of God manifest? Romans 3:22 says "the righteousness of God through faith in Jesus for all who believe..." and 3:28 says "For we hold that one is justified by faith apart from works of the law." These statements bring resolution to the prior condition mentioned; faith brings justification where man's works cannot. Justification by works and that by faith stand in contrast.

The assumption that Paul was seeking to make a statement about mankind's inability to believe in Jesus would change Paul's whole flow of thought. To take that interpretation you've got to conclude that rather than distinguishing between justification by the law and that by faith, Paul was making a somewhat isolated statement about man's inability to believe in Jesus (though Jesus is not at all in view in the Psalms passage or Romans 3:10–18) that is unrelated to Paul's conclusion in vv. 21–31. If the problem were that man is unable to believe, the resolution would have to be God somehow overcoming that inability in man to believe. We'd expect Paul to offer that resolution in the verses following his discussion of the problem. Instead, the verses following 3:10–18 discuss God's righteousness being manifested through faith/belief. If we assume that the problem is man's inability to believe, then this is no resolution at all; it doesn't matter that justification is by faith since we just established (in the Calvinist interpretation) that man is incapable of faith. Instead, the whole context much better fits the understanding that man cannot be saved by his own efforts under the law, but only through believing in Jesus. With this understanding of the passage, it makes sense for Paul to explain and illustrate (the quote in Rom. 3:10–18) the problem (man's inability to be justified by works), then provide the solution (justification by believing in Jesus).

There are a variety of verses that seem to indicate that some people (even those who aren't saved already) do seek God.

> And those who had set their hearts to seek the LORD God of Israel came after them from all the tribes of Israel to Jerusalem to sacrifice to the LORD, the God of their fathers. (2 Chron. 11:16)

> And he made from one man every nation of mankind to live on all the face of the earth, having determined allotted periods and the boundaries of their dwelling place, [27] that they should seek God, and perhaps feel their way toward him and find him. Yet he is actually not far from each one of us. (Acts 17:26–27)

> Seek the LORD while he may be found; call upon him while he is near; [7] let the wicked forsake his way, and the unrighteous man his thoughts; let him return to the LORD, that he may have compassion on him, and to our God, for he will abundantly pardon. (Isa. 55:6–7)

This doesn't invalidate the statement Paul (and the Psalmist) makes that "there is no one who seeks out God." However, in comparing Scripture with Scripture we do see that it's not as simple as saying that no one in any circumstance would ever turn to God (e.g., prevenient grace or not). We should also remember that while not everything about the passage Paul quotes from Psalm 14 is hyperbolic, there were certain hyperbolic elements (e.g., "all the evildoers who eat up my people as they eat bread"). David was contrasting "the fool" with "the generation of the righteous." So even in the quote's original context there is mention of those who are perhaps sensitive to God.

Taking the statement "there is no one who seeks out God" and claiming that this proves also that no one is capable of responding to God when He seeks them is a non sequitur (it does not follow logically). Consider the following example: the fact that you are unable to call the U.S. President (perhaps because you don't have his phone number) does not also mean that you would be unable to answer your phone if the President called you. We must agree that without God's initiation in the restoration of relationship with us, we could never be saved. We are wholly dependent upon His prevenient grace. Romans

3, however, has nothing to do with man's response to God's prevenient grace, only his natural disposition apart from God, which we agree on. It'd be wrong both biblically and logically to assume that because mankind can't save themselves by adherence to the law, they also can't admit their inability to keep the law and trust in the one who could keep it.

The truth is that God has taken the initiative to restore the relationship. He sent His Son Jesus to die on the cross for the sins of the whole world, gave us His Word, convicts the world, entrusts the church with the ministry of reconciliation, and draws all men to Himself.

> However, it was our sicknesses that He Himself bore, And our pains that He carried; Yet we ourselves assumed that He had been afflicted, Struck down by God, and humiliated. [5] But He was pierced for our offenses, He was crushed for our wrongdoings; The punishment for our well-being was laid upon Him, And by His wounds we are healed. [6] All of us, like sheep, have gone astray, Each of us has turned to his own way; But the Lord has caused the wrongdoing of us all to fall on Him. (Isa. 53:4–6)

> God our Savior, [4] who desires all people to be saved and to come to the knowledge of the truth. [5] For there is one God, and there is one mediator between God and men, the man Christ Jesus, [6] who gave himself as a ransom for all, which is the testimony given at the proper time. (1 Tim. 2:4–6)

> For the grace of God has appeared, bringing salvation for all people. (Tit. 2:11)

> "And I, if I am lifted up from the earth, will draw all men to Myself." (Jn. 12:32)

> "And when he comes, he will convict the world concerning sin and righteousness and judgment: [9] concerning sin, because they do not believe in me; [10] concerning

> righteousness, because I go to the Father, and you will see me no longer; [11] concerning judgment, because the ruler of this world is judged." (Jn. 16:8-11)
>
> Therefore put away all filthiness and rampant wickedness and receive with meekness the implanted word, which is able to save your souls. (Jas. 1:21)
>
> Romans 10:17, So faith comes from hearing, and hearing through the word of Christ. (Rom. 10:17)
>
> ...but these are written so that you may believe that Jesus is the Christ, the Son of God, and that by believing you may have life in his name. (Jn. 20:31)
>
> ...and how from childhood you have been acquainted with the sacred writings, which are able to make you wise for salvation through faith in Christ Jesus. (2 Tim. 3:15)
>
> Therefore, knowing the fear of the Lord, we persuade others. But what we are is known to God, and I hope it is known also to your conscience... [20] Therefore, we are ambassadors for Christ, as though God were making an appeal through us; we beg you on behalf of Christ, be reconciled to God. (2 Cor. 5:11, 20)
>
> And he entered the synagogue and for three months spoke boldly, reasoning and persuading them about the kingdom of God. (Acts 19:8)

Considering these and other passages, it seems quite reasonable to conclude that God has not only given the opportunity of salvation to all people, but even sought to persuade them to change their minds and believe in Jesus.

1 Corinthians 2:14

> But a natural person does not accept the things of the Spirit of God, for they are foolishness to him; and he cannot understand them, because they are spiritually discerned.

Again, the Calvinist rendering of this verse is that, without God making the determination for a person, no one would ever (in fact, could ever) respond to Jesus in faith. This is not the author's intended meaning for the text. In his first letter to the Corinthians, Paul was seeking to emphasize the contrast between worldly wisdom and that of God. While the Calvinist interpretation is that no unbeliever could accept Jesus because of their depravity, the context is best understood as distinguishing human wisdom from Spiritual truth.

Earlier in the book Paul mentions the "wisdom of the wise" (1:19), "wisdom of the world" (1:20), and the "wisdom of man" (2:5) or "human wisdom" (2:13). He teaches that those who rely on this as their source of what is true will regard the cross as foolish. For instance, "the world did not know God through wisdom" (1:21b) because Christ crucified is "folly to Gentiles" (1:23b). In other words, a reliance on lofty human ideas would not lead someone to accept Jesus. Though the "Greeks seek wisdom" (1:22b), the "foolishness of God is wiser than men" (1:25a). Human wisdom will lead a person nowhere. In fact, "For the word of the cross is folly to those who are perishing" (1:18). Along the same lines, Romans 8:6–8 says, "For to set the mind on the flesh is death, but to set the mind on the Spirit is life and peace. [7] For the mind that is set on the flesh is hostile to God, for it does not submit to God's law; indeed, it cannot. [8] Those who are in the flesh cannot please God." In contrast, to those who abandon human wisdom and instead trust in God and His Word, the things of God are powerful.

> ...but to us who are being saved it is the power of God... And because of him you are in Christ Jesus, who became to us wisdom from God, righteousness and sanctification and redemption. (1 Cor. 1:18, 30)

> ...and how from childhood you have been acquainted with the sacred writings, which are able to make you wise for salvation through faith in Christ Jesus. 16 All Scripture is breathed out by God and profitable for teaching, for reproof, for correction, and for training in righteousness. (2 Tim. 3:15–16)

Paul's purpose for getting into this discussion of wisdom was to point out that He was sent to preach the gospel "not with words of eloquent wisdom, lest the cross of Christ be emptied of its power" (1:17b). Indeed, he "decided to know nothing among [them] except Jesus Christ and him crucified" (2:2) because Christ is "the power of God and the wisdom of God" (1:24b) and the "word of the cross" is "the power of God" to those who are saved (1:18). All of this points to the truth that Paul wanted the faith of His recipients to be from the working of the Spirit and the power of God rather than lofty words of human wisdom. In fact, in 1 Corinthians 2:5 he says that he focused on Jesus Christ and Him crucified "so that your faith might not rest in the wisdom of men but in the power of God."

First Corinthians 3:1–3, the passage which follows this mention in 2:14, clarifies that Paul's recipients were both believers ("brothers" in 3:1) and "people of the flesh" (3:1) who were "behaving only in a human way" (3:3). Because they were doing so, and the natural person can't understand the things of God which are spiritually discerned (2:14), Paul had to address them as "infants in Christ" (3:1) and feed them "with milk" (3:2). Was the problem that these believers had an inability to respond to God? Of course not, for they were believers. Instead, they were depending on worldly wisdom rather than God. If we did assume that 2:14 meant that people in general are incapable of believing in Jesus, we'd have to assume Paul's recipients were incapable of growth spiritually (which would raise additional questions). This is never the case for believers, so we can reject the idea that the inability of "the natural man" to understand the things of God is not because of their position as people of the flesh but because they settle for human wisdom. Furthermore, the fact that reliance on worldly wisdom causes people to see the cross as foolishness does not at all mean that man is incapable of relying on anything other than human wisdom.

Ephesians 1:3–14

> Blessed be the God and Father of our Lord Jesus Christ, who has blessed us in Christ with every spiritual blessing in the heavenly places, 4 even as he chose us in him before the foundation of the world, that we should be holy and blameless before him. In love 5 he predestined us for adoption to himself as sons through Jesus Christ, according to the purpose of his will, 6 to the praise of his glorious grace, with which he has blessed us in the Beloved. 7 In him we have redemption through his blood, the forgiveness of our trespasses, according to the riches of his grace, 8 which he lavished upon us, in all wisdom and insight 9 making known to us the mystery of his will, according to his purpose, which he set forth in Christ 10 as a plan for the fullness of time, to unite all things in him, things in heaven and things on earth. 11 In him we have obtained an inheritance, having been predestined according to the purpose of him who works all things according to the counsel of his will, 12 so that we who were the first to hope in Christ might be to the praise of his glory. 13 In him you also, when you heard the word of truth, the gospel of your salvation, and believed in him, were sealed with the promised Holy Spirit, 14 who is the guarantee of our inheritance until we acquire possession of it, to the praise of his glory.

Ephesians 1 is one of the most prominent passages used in support of Calvinist ideas. Their interpretation leans on verse 4 in saying that God determined who would be saved. The phrase "he chose us in him" serves as the crux of the difference in interpretations, as it could be understood as meaning that God chose who would be "in Him", or that He chose what would be true of those who are "in Him." The context seems to render the latter as the most reasonable understanding. Indeed, the primary emphasis here, as elsewhere, surrounding election is the ultimate destiny of those who are "in Christ," not the mechanistic selection of who would be "in Christ."

No biblical author at any point clearly explains the mechanics of the Calvinist idea that God determines who would be saved. The only verses in the Bible where the Greek *ἐκλεκτός* (*eklektos*) is used to refer to what's true of believers in general rather than to refer to a specific person or group (not teaching universal soteriology) are Colossians 3:12, and 1 Peter 2:9. In both Colossians 3:12 ("Put on then, as God's chosen ones…") and 1 Peter 2:9 ("But you are a chosen race, a royal priesthood, a holy nation…") the use of the word "chosen" (*ἐκλεκτός*, *eklektos*) serves as an adjective describing the letter's recipients, but says nothing about the particulars of election (neither verse tells us how God chooses, why He does, etc.). Ephesians 1:4, then, is arguably the clearest instance in Scripture for the Calvinist claim of election; God determining salvation.

> Even in Ephesians 1, though, the message that God chooses who will and will not be saved is unclear. The emphasis is on the spiritual blessings true of believers. The phrases "in him," "in Christ," and "in the beloved" are used frequently (eight times) in this passage signaling the connection between the blessings and the union with Jesus. The very use of the phrase "in Him" is to remind us that all these spiritual blessings are tied to our union with Christ. In other words, all these spiritual blessings are true of us because we are in Christ, and for no other reason; in fact, they can't be true of us outside of Christ. We'd be inconsistent in saying that the use of "in Him" in verse 4 pertains to how people become saved, but that the rest of the references to being "in Him" pertain to things that are true of people who are already saved.

The clearest evidence we see in God's Word- regarding how a person is saved- points, instead, to human belief in the person and work of Jesus as the causal element. Even in Ephesians 1, the clearest statement regarding the mechanics of salvation pertains not to God's election, but to man's belief.

> In Him you also, when you heard the word of truth, the gospel of your salvation, and believed in Him, were sealed with the promised Holy Spirit. (Eph. 1:13)

This verse is clear, and in line with what we know from elsewhere in God's Word. People are positioned in Christ when they believe in Him. With that in mind, we can understand Ephesians 1:4 as teaching that God determined that those who are in Him "should be holy and blameless before Him," as well as experience several other spiritual blessings. For further clarity, consider an illustration. Two coaches, coach A and coach B, chose before the beginning of their season (in fact even before anyone was on their team) that their team would be well-conditioned. The fact that coach A would personally select each member of his team and coach B, on the other hand, would openly invite everyone to join his team, is irrelevant concerning the choice they both made to train and condition their teams. That choice didn't concern who would be on their team, but instead, the ultimate plan each coach had for their team. Similarly, the fact that God chose the ultimate destiny of those who are "in Him" is irrelevant, in itself, to the determination (on either God's or man's side) of who would be "in Him." That was simply not Paul's focus. The reliance on Ephesians 1:4 as a proof for God selecting who is saved, then, is at least a stretch, whether the idea is true or not elsewhere.

Romans 8:28–30

> And we know that for those who love God all things work
> together for good, for those who are called according to his
> purpose. 29 For those whom he foreknew he also
> predestined to be conformed to the image of his Son, in
> order that he might be the firstborn among many brothers.
> 30 And those whom he predestined he also called, and those
> whom he called he also justified, and those whom he
> justified he also glorified.

Similar to Ephesians 1, the common Calvinist interpretation offered for this passage is that God determines the salvation of men. There are several potential interpretations we might take for this section, but I've concluded that both the understanding that God elected individuals based on foresight of their faith and that God foreordained that certain individuals would be saved can be ruled out as less reasonable alternatives.

In verse 28, Paul says that those who God foreknew were also predestined to be conformed to the image of His Son. Since not everyone will share that destiny, we can assume that those whom God "foreknew" were a group of people, rather than everyone. The word, then, isn't a reference to God's prescience- His knowing all things past, present, and future. Those subscribing to the "foresight of faith" view hold that particular group as those who God had known would believe in Him. On the other hand, proponents of the "foreordination" camp believe the group is a reference to those God determined to save (the elect). Both views require reading into the text and assuming a meaning which seems outside the emphasis of the author.

The concept of foreknowledge (προγινώσκω, *proginōskō*; πρόγνωσις, *prognōsis*) in Scripture most commonly conveys God's relational knowledge. Simply put, those God had relationally known beforehand (from times past). We could read Romans 8:29 as "those whom he'd known beforehand, he predestined to be conformed to the image of His Son…" Once again, the emphasis of predestination is the destiny of the believer (ultimate glorification), rather than the mechanics of God determining who would believe. There is just no way to prove that Paul meant to teach the Calvinist concept of election; a far cry from the idea that the passage clearly teaches it. In fact, such an interpretation would be foreign to the contextual flow.

Paul was, in Romans 8, trying to encourage his recipients, who were suffering.

> …fellow heirs with Christ, provided we suffer with him in order that we may also be glorified with him. [18] For I consider that the sufferings of this present time are not worth comparing with the glory that is to be revealed to us… [23] And not only the creation, but we ourselves, who have the firstfruits of the Spirit, groan inwardly as we wait

> eagerly for adoption as sons, the redemption of our bodies. (Rom. 8:17b–18, 23)

Then in verse 28 he reminds his readers that "God causes all things to work together for good to those who love God, to those who are called according to His purpose." Using the word "for," to link verse 29 with that concept, Paul then explains that those who God has known beforehand were predestined, and that the chain resulting in glorification was so certain that things which are yet future could be spoken of in past tense. He was seeking to bolster the Romans in their present trials by pointing their focus to their eventual and eternal glorification. In the verses after this passage, he drives the point home.

> "What then shall we say to these things? If God is for us, who is against us? [32] He who did not spare His own Son, but delivered Him over for us all, how will He not also with Him freely give us all things?... [35] Who will separate us from the love of Christ?... [37] But in all these things we overwhelmingly conquer through Him who loved us. (Rom. 8:31–32, 35a, 37)

None of these passages, which are arguably the most pro-Calvinist in Scripture, explicitly teach the Calvinist ideas that God determines salvation or that man would never choose to change their mind and believe in Jesus, if given the choice. In fact, evidence suggests that these ideas were foreign to the emphasis of the biblical authors. Augustine apparently did arrive at this conclusion based primarily on philosophical presuppositions; and without the grounding support of such passages, philosophy is ultimately the system's greatest strength.

REASON AND CALVINISM

There is a difference between inscrutability and logical inconsistency (contradiction/impossibility). Something that is inscrutable has reached the limit of how far logic can go in helping us explore that topic. It has an illogical element; it is beyond/outside of our ability to reduce it to logical consideration. For instance, the fact that God exists eternally as one God in three persons is inscrutable. We cannot employ reasoning to comprehend that idea much further than that statement. Just because it's inscrutable, however, doesn't mean it's illogical. To say that God is one God in three Gods would be illogical, but the nature of God is such that it is not illogical to say that there is one God in three persons. Instead, something is logically incoherent when, within the realm of logical consideration (prior to the point of inscrutability), reasoning reckons an idea impossible for one reason or another. For instance, there could never be a married bachelor, because those are two mutually exclusive states of being, only one can be true at a time. There is no speculation or inscrutability in this scenario; it's not the case that such a thing might exist in another possible world (or somewhere in this one that we don't know about), it is logically impossible, and we may confidently deny that married bachelors even could exist. My contention is that the Calvinist ideas that 1) God determines salvation and that 2) people, if given the determination, would never choose to believe in Jesus, are invalid (logically impossible) given what is clear concerning God, and should therefore be rejected.

On an individual basis, it is logically necessary to conclude that either God determines salvation or the individuals themselves determine salvation. Trying to claim that, for the same individual, both God and man determined the person's salvation is logically impossible because it holds two mutually exclusive things to be true simultaneously (like the concept of a married bachelor). Please recognize that this does not mean that it's impossible for both God and man to choose the same thing regarding man's belief; only that it's impossible for them both to have determination. To illustrate, consider a scenario in which both, hypothetically, have determination, and they make different decisions. Because they both have determination, neither has the final authority (the "last word") in the decision and they remain in a stalemate, which proves that neither of them ever truly had determination in the first place.

In His sovereignty, God has the ultimate authority and power in determining salvation, and the only way for man to have it at all is for God to relinquish His right to determine and leave the determination to man; at which point He forfeits His ability to overturn man's decision (or they could never have been said to possess the determination). From these core concepts, we can conclude that the following are the only logical possibilities when considering who determines salvation:

1. God determines the salvation of all individuals; some to believe and some to reject Him.
2. Every individual determines their own salvation; some to believe and some to reject Him.
3. God determines the salvation of some individuals, while all others determine their own.

On the Idea that God Determines Salvation for All Individuals

Many Calvinists hold to the first explanation; that God determines salvation for everyone. Because not everyone is saved, implicit and required in this view is the idea that God determines that some people would reject Him; regardless of whether they'd accept Him if they had determination for themselves. There are several reasons for why this isn't a reasonable conclusion.

First, we know that God's desired will is that all people would be saved. 2 Peter 3:9 says, "The Lord is not slow about His promise, as some count slowness, but is patient toward you, not wishing for any to perish but for all to come to repentance," and 1 Timothy 2:3b–4, "God our Savior, who desires all men to be saved and to come to the knowledge of the truth." If God is the determiner of salvation for all individuals, the only explanation for why not all people are saved is that God doesn't want them to be. But since God is immutable (He does not change), it would be unreasonable to assume that He eternally and simultaneously holds the contradictory desires that, on one hand, all people be saved, and on the other, not all people be saved. The conclusion that, at least for everyone who rejects God, He has given individuals determination of their own salvation, is logically necessary to maintain a Biblical view of God.

Old Testament saints living under the economy of law were incapable of keeping the law's demands, as the New Testament authors make clear, and were yet held accountable for whether they did. From this we see that God holding people accountable for something they have no ability to fulfill is consistent with His justice. Is that the most reasonable explanation, however, of what is happening when someone rejects God (in the salvation context)? Is the most reasonable explanation that God died on the cross and presents the Gospel universally, the acceptance of which gives eternal life, but determines that some people won't have the ability to accept Him? I would argue that it's not. The inability to keep the law is quite different than the inability to believe in Jesus. Everyone in the human race (except Jesus, of course) inherits a sin nature and inevitably deserves separation from God because of Adam's sin. Romans 5:12 and 18a, say "Therefore, just as through one man sin entered into the world, and death through sin, and so death spread to all men, because all sinned… So then as through one transgression there resulted condemnation to all men." As fallen people the law could never have provided salvation. In fact, one of the reasons God gave Israel the law was to expose their sin and inability to be saved on their own accord! Christ came to, among other things, provide people with everything necessary for them to spend eternity in relationship with Him (redemption, propitiation, reconciliation, etc.). If even just one person remained unable to believe in Jesus, it would be because God determined that the effects of the saving work of Jesus on the cross would never be potential for them. They would remain unable to believe in Jesus because God so determined; yet they would be accountable based on whether they believed (Jn. 3:18). In that sense, the sin of Adam, which spread to all humanity (again, minus Jesus), was more comprehensive in its effect than the death of Jesus; an unbiblical and unreasonable concept. While this may be logically possible, the notion that God, who is love and desires for all people to enter relationship with Him for eternity, seems vehemently contrary to His character. Far more reasonable is the perception that the death of Christ on the cross created the potential for all people to believe and so be saved. Adding to that conclusion is the fact that God's Word teaches the principles that people are held accountable at varying degrees based on the amount of revelation they're exposed to (e.g., Mt. 11:20–24), and that infants are not culpable until the "age of accountability" because of their lack of ability to determine salvation for themselves prior to that point.

Claiming that God determines who will and will not be in relationship with Himself inevitably reduces the meaning in that relationship to that of mere utility. The commonly used illustration, that God determining some to be saved is just as meaningful as a couple determining to adopt a child who has no choice in that matter, is a faulty one because it's fundamentally different from what it's used to explain (God's relationship with man). The example begins with free creatures in an already meaningful relationship (humans with other humans), and in this circumstance. Instead, a relationship between God and man in which God controls at least some of what man will do is more like that of a computer engineer with a computer. The engineer may design and program however they like, and the computer will do exactly what it's been determined to. Is this a meaningful relationship? No. Not beyond the utilitarian sense that the computer can be used for the purposes of the computer engineer. While this, too, is a possible scenario, the most reasonable understanding of reality, based on the character of God and the Word of God, is that God gave man freedom so that our relationship with Him would be incredibly meaningful. C.S. Lewis, in *Mere Christianity*, put this concept quite eloquently when he said:

> Is this state of affairs in accordance with God's will or not? If it is, He is a strange God you will say; and if it is not, how can anything happen contrary to the will of a being with absolute power. But anyone who has been in authority knows how a thing can be in accordance with your will in one way and not in another. It may be quite sensible for a mother to say to the children 'I'm not going to go and make you tidy the schoolroom every night. You've got to learn to keep it tidy on your own.' Then she goes up one night and finds the teddy bear and the ink and the French grammar all lying in the grate. That is against her will. She

> would prefer the children be tidy. On the other hand, it is her will which has left the children free to be untidy… That is not what you willed, but your will has made it possible. It is probably the same in the universe. God created things which had free will. That means creatures which can go either wrong or right. Some people think they can imagine a creature which was free but had no possibility of going wrong. I cannot. If a thing is free to be good, it is also free to be bad. And free will is what has made evil possible. Why, then, did God give them free will? Because free will, though it makes evil possible, is also the only thing that makes possible any love or goodness or joy worth having. A world of automata – of creatures that worked like machines--would hardly be worth creating. The happiness which God designs for His higher creatures is the happiness of being freely, voluntarily united to Him and to each other in an ecstasy of love and delight compared with which the most rapturous love between a man and a woman on this earth is mere milk and water. And for that they must be free.

The idea that God passed the determination of salvation for at least some individuals to them is not at all contradictory to His sovereignty. God's Word is clear that He, alone, is God; holy, omnipotent, omniscient, eternal, and so much more. He may do as He pleases (Psa. 115:3). This does not necessitate, however, that He always meticulously controls everything that ever happens. In fact, if that were true then we would have to resign to the conclusion that He is the author and orchestrator of evil. Instead, God may permit man and angels to determine things on their own; the most reasonable and Biblical conclusion. A.W. Tozer, in *The Knowledge of the Holy*, put it this way:

> God sovereignly decreed that man should be free to exercise moral choice, and man from the beginning has fulfilled that decree by making his choice between good and evil. When he chooses to do evil, he does not thereby

countervail the sovereign will of God but fulfills it, inasmuch as the eternal decree decided not which choice the man should make but that he should be free to make it. If in His absolute freedom God has willed to give man limited freedom, who is there to stay His hand or say, 'What doest thou?' Man's will is free because God is sovereign. A God less than sovereign could not bestow moral freedom upon His creatures. He would be afraid to do so.

On the Idea that God Determines the Salvation of Some Individuals, while All Others Determine their Own

	Of all whom God doesn't determine, some believe, and others reject Him.	All whom God doesn't determine believe.	All whom God doesn't determine reject Him.
God determines that some will believe and that some will reject Him.	a	b	c
God determines that some will believe; not that anyone will reject Him.	d	e	f
God determines that some will reject Him; not that anyone will believe.	g	h	i

Within the scope of the third possibility, which is more philosophically sophisticated, there are nine distinct scenarios (illustrated in the following table). To best understand the table, read the first column first (the rows that begin "God determines…"), and then the rest of the column headers in row one. Remember that each of these scenarios assume that God determines the salvation of some but bestows the determination of their own salvation to others.

If we reject the ideas that everyone is saved (universalism) and that no-one is saved, then we can rule out e and i. Above we discussed the issues with the idea that God determined that individuals (even just one) would reject Him and spend an eternity separated from Him in hell. Rejecting that concept, we can also rule out *a*, *b*, *c*, *g*, and *h*. After removing these options, the most reasonable remaining explanations include *d*) God determines that some believe in Him, and of individuals who are given their own determination, some believe in Him and others reject Him, or *f*: God determines that some believe in Him, and all individuals who are given their own determination reject Him.

The first of these options is logically possible but doesn't represent the Calvinist view because it necessarily claims that man can believe when left with their own determination. The most reasonable Calvinist explanation, then, is that God determines that some believe in Him, and all individuals who are given their own determination reject Him. Let's examine this idea further. To say that all individuals who are given determination of their own salvation (the ability to choose whether to believe in Jesus) reject Him can mean one of two things. Either everyone rejects Him by necessity (because they're incapable of accepting Him; accepting Him isn't a potential option), or everyone rejects Him by circumstance, meaning that individuals may potentially believe in Him (and perhaps do in certain possible worlds), but given the specific circumstances that exist in the actual world, none have believed in Him. Both are problematic.

First, if no one can believe in Jesus when given determination, we must conclude that God, Himself, is incapable of persuading a free individual to accept Him and that the only way anyone will believe in

Him is for God never to give them the freedom to choose but to somehow make the choice for them. This idea implies that the combined forces of human depravity, Satanic/demonic influence, and the world are so powerful in swaying man's determination of whether or not to believe in Jesus that man would never accept Him, and that there is literally nothing God can do (short of coercion, the usage of which He would have already forfeited in giving man the determination) to even provide a degree of influence in an individual's life that would create the possibility of them changing their mind. In this context, saying that no individual ever would (in any possible world) is effectively equivalent to saying that no individual ever could. Such an idea- again, that God would be incapable of persuading people to accept Him without having to coerce them into doing so- seems absurd.

The second option states that people can believe in Jesus when given determination, but it so happens in this world that no one has. In other words, in some possible worlds (with different circumstances) people who have determination of their own salvation choose to believe in Jesus, but not in the actual world (though they possess the potential to accept Him, just the same). While this view is logically possible (in fact, the most logically consistent of all options), holding it requires rejecting Calvinist interpretations of passages concerning human depravity (e.g., John 6:44 and Romans 3:10-12), which claim (at a minimum) that individuals would never believe in Jesus if given determination. In short, this is not a Calvinist view because it rejects the Calvinist rendering of human depravity.

So we see that, with the Calvinist rendering of human depravity, there is no logically consistent answer to the question of "Who determines salvation; God or the individual?" Instead, the only logical answer to that question is that God has given all individuals determination, for themselves, of whether they will believe in Jesus or reject Him. This idea also happens to be consistent with the most reasonable understanding of Biblical passages; the interpretation we come to when applying sound principles of exegesis. Furthermore, if determination of the salvation of all individuals rests with them, then the mere fact that some people are believers is sufficient to disprove the Calvinist rendering of human depravity, which states that, left to their determination, man would never believe in Jesus. Ultimately, neither the Calvinist idea of election nor depravity are reasonable.

On The Idea That God Has Given All Individuals Determination of their Own Salvation

By process of elimination, the idea that God has given everyone the ability to believe in Jesus or reject Him is most reasonable (arguably the only logical possibility). One of the biggest problems Calvinists tend to have with this is the implication that man is involved in their own salvation. Under this view, not only is an individual involved in their salvation, but their act of belief is also the causal determinant of their salvation; though of course we'd all recognize that causal determination couldn't have been possible without God. To the Calvinist, this is much too high a view of man and far too low a view of God in salvation. The view is logically coherent, so the primary objection is instead theological; based on the apparent contradiction between the concept and the nature of God and doctrine of salvation. Calvinists may even so oppose the idea that man could be involved in salvation that they consider it logically necessary to adhere to the view that God wholly determines salvation and man has absolutely no part in it (ironically, while ignoring the logical issues with that view).

In answering this objection, I would point out both the distinction between being the causal determiner and deserving credit, and the distinction between works and faith. Simply being the causal determiner (last actor that makes a particular thing happen; without which the thing wouldn't have happened) of something doesn't mean you may take credit for the event. In fact, in some cases involving gifts between multiple parties, the causal determiner can't be said to contribute to the gift whatsoever, only to the existence of the relationship; since the giver can't (in human contexts) coerce the recipient to receive the gift. Imagine, for instance, that a stranger gave you $50 when they heard it was your birthday. The acceptance of that gift, on your part, is the causal determinant of you possessing the $50, and yet your decision to receive the gift didn't contribute any additional money. You accepted the gift, yet you still have just the $50 the stranger gave you. No one could say that you earned that money, but only that it was given to you. Similarly, God offers everyone the gift of eternal life (relationship with Him), and our acceptance of it by faith does absolutely nothing to contribute to what God has done to save us. It couldn't be said that we earned salvation in any way, only that God freely provided it for us. With the stark contrast Scripture paints between works and faith, it seems unreasonable to equate the two in claiming that an individual's exercise of faith would be scandalous because they could never earn their salvation on their own. The Bible never once portrays faith as a means of earning one's salvation; only as the means by which man humbly repents, admitting their sin and trusting in the person and work of Jesus alone to save them. In fact, a person's boasting in their belief, as though worthy of credit for their salvation, would be to misunderstand and devalue the significance of Jesus and His offer of eternal life almost completely. For any meaningful relationship between two persons to exist, there must have been at least one determined action from both parties. In the case of human beings in relationship with God, it just so happens that God has made all the necessary provisions, as He alone could, and left to individuals only the determination of whether they would enter the relationship with Him.

CONCLUSION

History has left us with relatively great clarity regarding where the ideas of divine determinism and man's inability to believe in Jesus came from. Augustine came to such conclusions in opposition to the heretical teaching of Pelagius while seeking to reconcile his theological framework, which led to at least a partial infusion of ideas from the pagan philosophies he'd been familiar with prior to his conversion. The burden of proof, then, falls on adherents of these ideas to prove that every one of the other early church fathers and many after him were wrong, and convince us that Augustine, while infusing such a large degree of His fatalistic former philosophy into his theology, was right.

In holding Calvinist presuppositions under the microscope, evidence favors the notion that the cycle of claiming biblical support for these ideas but deriving that support primarily from presuppositions began not with sound exegesis, but with reading a philosophical structure into the text. Close examination of even the strongest support passages indicates that these ideas were far from the emphasis of what the biblical authors were trying to communicate. Instead, in each case there are other, more reasonable conclusions as to the author's most likely intended meaning. It seems that the only way we'd surmise that those ideas were supported biblically is by approaching verses while already presupposing their meaning. Lastly, even at a philosophical level, which I've asserted is the foundation and ultimate strength of Calvinism, the system falls apart due to logical incoherence. The presuppositions themselves require affirming a chain of logic which is sequentially unreasonable. Ultimately then, God does not determine the salvation of mankind but has given such determination to us (and not to some, but to all mankind). We are able to accept His offer of eternal life and so be saved, not because of our own goodness, but solely because of His prior actions on our behalf.

DOMINION

A SURVEY OF THE MEDIATORIAL KINGDOM

Pastor E Dane Rogers

Introduction

God has many purposes in history which work together to reveal His insurmountable glory; one such purpose is to rule over His Creation through His human image-bearers (Gen. 1:26–28). Because of this, the expectation of a physical and earthly kingdom never disappears from the pages of scripture. It pulsates continually in the background of God's interactions with mankind throughout the Biblical record. Despite the pervasive Old Testament preoccupation with a literal and physical kingdom, many have come to interpret the kingdom references in the New Testament as a spiritual kingdom. One cause of this faulty interpretation has been the dislocation of Old Testament prophecies from their New Testament fulfillment. It is important to interpret the kingdom in the New Testament in light of Old Testament revelation. This survey traces God's kingdom program from inception to fulfillment as revealed in scripture. For the purposes of this study, we must begin by defining and distinguishing the mediatorial kingdom.

Distinctions

To competently discuss any subject, we must begin by establishing a common vocabulary. This will require both definition and distinction to specify what exactly is meant by "mediatorial kingdom." First, the mediatorial kingdom is distinct from and subservient to the universal kingdom. The universal kingdom is that reign of God which exists in transcendence to the created universe; it is not constrained by time, space, or matter; it is the eternal domain of God, over which He has always and will always be sovereign. "Universal" may even be a reductive description of God's sovereign rule, since God's rule is eternal, not restricted to the existence of a created universe. It is precisely God's distinction from His creation which qualifies Him alone to sit unchallenged as sovereign over the universe. To even begin to compete with God's sovereignty, one must himself be an uncreated being. Thus, this universal and eternal kingdom of God has never been subverted from God's sovereign will.

Gentry writes this of God's eternal rule over the universal kingdom,

> Scripture begins by declaring that God, as Creator and triune Lord, is the sovereign ruler and King of the universe. In this important sense, the entire universe is God's kingdom since he is at present Lord and King. From the Bible's opening, God is introduced and identified as the all-powerful Lord who created the universe by His word, while He Himself is uncreated, independent, self-existent, self-sufficient, and in need of nothing outside Himself… He rules with perfect power, knowledge, and righteousness… He is the King, and the entire universe is His kingdom. This truth is nicely captured by Psalm 103:19: "The Lord has established His throne in heaven, and His kingdom rules over all" (NIV).[11]

The "mediatorial kingdom" was the choice term of Alva J. McClain to speak of the delegated rule of God on earth. McClain defines the mediatorial kingdom as,

> …the rule of God through a divinely chosen representative who not only speaks and acts for God but also represents the people before God… a rule which has especial

---

[11] Peter J. Gentry and Stephen J. Wellum, *Kingdom through Covenant: A Biblical-Theological Understanding of the Covenants*, 2nd ed. (Wheaton, IL: Crossway, 2018), 648-649. A thorough handling of the distinction of the universal kingdom can be found in Alva J. McClain, *The Greatness of the Kingdom: An Inductive Study of the Kingdom of God*, (Winona Lake, IN: BMH, 1959), 19-36.

reference to the earth; and... having as its mediatorial ruler one who is always a member of the human race.[12]

This is an agreeable definition, however what McClain has termed the "mediatorial" kingdom is the ideal state of that domain; for most of its existence, the mediatorial kingdom has not operated regularly. Thus, I propose confining the ideal state of the mediatorial kingdom to the term "theocratic kingdom," being the union of mediatorial dominion and theocratic rule. It can well be said that the mediatorial kingdom *ought to be*, *has been* and *will be* ruled theocratically, but in the history of the mediatorial kingdom it has seldom operated as a theocracy. For precisely this reason, it is beneficial to distinguish between the regular and irregular operation of the mediatorial kingdom. In this survey, the term "mediatorial" kingdom, and its derivatives, (i.e., mediatorial rule, mediator, etc.) will constitute the dominion over which humanity is responsible to rule, as was bestowed upon Adam at creation, and has been the general prerogative of humanity to govern throughout history. The mediatorial kingdom is man's rule over the whole world, but it is only *theocratic* so long as it administers God's will over creation through human administration.

The regular intended operation of the mediatorial kingdom is to execute God's will over creation by means of a human administrator. This is the theocratic rule of the mediatorial kingdom. However, not all theocracies are mediatorial since the domain of the mediatorial kingdom encompasses all of creation. For the mediatorial kingdom to function theocratically, it requires several things: global influence, including over its inhabitants; divine revelation of God's will and the mechanisms to implement it; and the localized presence of God.[13]

---

[12] McClain, 41.

[13] The mediatorial kingdom has existed as a theocracy historically in Eden where God manifested Himself among His administrators (Gen. 3:8). Furthermore, while God's presence was manifested in Israel in the form of the Shekinah glory (Ex. 40:34), from the time of the exodus, until the exile (Ezek. 10–11) when the glory departed from the temple, Israel's government was structured to implement God's will over the land and the inhabitants of Israel, but it was only a global superpower for a brief period under Solomon. Israel's

While Israel was a theocracy from its inception and has, to greater or lesser degrees, continued to exist as a form of theocracy, its theocratic government is not interminably paired with the mediatorial kingdom. The mediatorial kingdom is possessed by all humanity, and its throne is mediated by the dominant superpower over the globe. Babylon, Greece, Rome, Egypt, and Assyria have all occupied the throne of the mediatorial kingdom in ages past, but only Israel has been both theocratic and mediatorial. The mediatorial kingdom depends on the alignment of mankind's will while they steward the earth, either on behalf of God and His will, or on behalf of Satan's opposing will. This is the cosmic rule which Satan exercises over creation today through human administrators.

Satan has as his goal the administration of his own will over God's mediatorial kingdom, thus placing himself in a position which reflects God's sovereignty over creation. Satan's plans are moving toward the imposition of his own will through the headship of a singular human ruler, the false messiah, who will administer Satan's will from Babylon while Satan's presence is manifested on earth. This is a demonic replica of God's plan to place His own Son, the king of God's choosing, over creation as the perfect Godman, who will rule with righteousness and administer God's will over creation in the Messianic kingdom. This survey traces the program of this mediatorial kingdom as God works through history to wrest control away from Satan and restore it to its rightful ruler, Jesus the Messiah, King of kings and Lord of lords.

This is the goal of history, and the world cannot pass away until the Messiah is enthroned as the king over creation. Ryrie said it this way: "In the same *arena* where Satan has reigned, Christ will be victorious."[14] The world cannot pass away until God, in his purpose for creation, has been vindicated and glorified in Jesus the King.

---

historical kingdom has been at best a microcosm of the future theocratic kingdom.

[14] Charles Caldwell Ryrie, *Basic Theology: A Popular Systematic Guide to Understanding Biblical Truth* (Chicago, IL: Moody Press, 1999), 174. (Italics added).

Universal Kingdom of God
Eternal Transcendent Sovereignty

Mediatorial Kingdom
Temporal Dominion over Creation

Theocratic Rule (God's positive will)	**Cosmic Rule (God's permissive will)**
• God's will mediated through human administration	• Satan's will (to oppose God's will) mediated through human administration
• Regular (intended) state of mediatorial kingdom	• Irregular (corrupt) state of mediatorial kingdom
• Centralized authority: o Ante-diluvian: Eden o Post-diluvian: Jerusalem o Millennium: New Jerusalem	• Centralized authority: o Ante-diluvian: City of Enoch? o Post-diluvian: Babel/Babylon o Post-Millennium: Gog/Magog
• Ultimately victorious	• Ultimately vanquished
Goal: Messianic Kingdom	*Goal: Satanic Kingdom of the False Messiah*

The Mediatorial Kingdom in the Old Testament

Eden

Despite man's creation in the image of God, it would be a gross misunderstanding to extrapolate from this any doctrine of ontological continuity between God and man. Humanity, by nature of being a created entity, is already irreconcilably and eternally distinguished from God. No elevation of man, nor demotion of God, can possibly bridge that barrier. While God can add to Himself a created nature, he cannot forfeit His eternal preexistence. God will always be the uncaused cause of all things, and although God's creation of humanity reflects His own eternality—having been created to exist into the eternal future—humanity will always have a point of beginning, preceded by non-existence, while God has no beginning and no end and is not preceded by non-existence.

We are not surprised to find that God's planning period for creation predates the creation event. Though in progressive revelation we are first presented with God's rationale for creating mankind in Genesis 1:26, later scripture reveals that God had as His goal the incarnation of His own Son to inherit the throne of creation (Eph. 1, Rev. 5). Humanity was created distinct, bearing God's own image, so that the second person of the Trinity could take on a form that was suitable to His own nature. While we reflect God's character in finite portions—knowledge, complex language, moral agency, creativity, love, etc.—even our physical bodies are designed to reflect Him. Though scripture often attributes to God anthropomorphisms—describing God by means of human characteristics—we must recognize that this is only possible because we ourselves were designed as theomorphic beings. We were made in His image not only to understand Him, but also because He Himself planned to possess a human body. As we begin, we must note that Adam was not the goal of creation. Rather, creation has had as its goal from the beginning that descendant which would come from Adam's race, the Godman who would rule over creation in perfect faithfulness to God's will.

God created the earth to be a kingdom and installed Adam's race as creation's administrators through whom He would rule the world. Adam, as the federal and seminal head of the race was responsible to rule in subjection to God's will. God revealed this purpose in Genesis 1:26, and He communicated this role to Adam verbally in Genesis 1:28. "God blessed them; and God said to them, 'Be fruitful and multiply, and fill the earth, and subdue it; and rule over the fish of the sea and over the birds of the sky and over every living thing that moves on the earth.'"[15] Thus, Adam became the first theocratic administrator and mediatorial king, responsible to rule faithfully over God's creation.

Productive Institutions: Labor, Marriage, Family

God organized the social structure of humanity from its very beginning, providing mankind with three divine institutions for participating in the production of Godly society. These institutions are labor, marriage, and family. These reflect God's own activity of creation. Man was to observe God's general revelation in the nature around him and interpret it by means of God's special revelation. The world which Adam entered was uncultivated (Gen. 2:5-6), and God's first recorded act after Adam's creation (v. 7) was to cultivate a garden (vv. 8-14) and to place him in it, with the purpose of reflecting His own activity of cultivation (v. 15). Rest is also part of the reflected order of God's labor, in which He enjoys the fruits of labor. In man's mediatorial role, he is to reflect God's own ethic of productive and responsible labor over creation. His role is as caring steward, not abusive overlord. The built-in ability which plants and animals possess (Gen. 1:11, 22) enable the man to participate in God's productive work, spreading over the whole earth as God had intended (Gen. 1:28). Adam's most basic means of reflecting God's creative glory in the garden was through horticulture and animal husbandry.

The second divine institution was marriage. God revealed that man's solitude was not part of His will, and thus was not "good" as the other completed elements of creation had been. God showed Adam his need for fellowship through general revelation (Gen. 2:19–22 cf. 1:27) and special revelation (Gen. 2:18). Adam observed God work and understood what He did through divine interpretation (v. 23) and the institution of marriage was implemented (v. 24). Marriage would promote Godly society through procreation as well as fellowship (i.e., spiritual & physical communion). Beyond man's labor of horticulture

---

[15] Scripture citations are from the *New American Standard Bible: 1995 Update* (La Habra, CA: The Lockman Foundation, 1995).

and animal husbandry, he has been given the ability to share in God's work of creating and raising generations of humanity. The reproductive capacity of the woman was also God's installed means of entering into human society as a human to inherit the throne of this earth. The union of man and woman reflected God's capacity and glory in fellowship, though in a finite way.

The third divine institution was family. Through the procreation of the human race, the man and the woman were to instruct their children, just as God had instructed them, and delegate rule over creation. God's glory was to be seen in sharing His labor with free moral agents as those created beings obey Him of their own free will. His glory would be demonstrated to mankind as they experienced the responsibility of creating, instructing, and nurturing. However, His ultimate glory would be revealed in the incarnation of His own Son into the human race—the promise of a Seed, God's manifest glory on earth.

Failure to Administer God's Will

Genesis 3 records Adam's failure as theocratic administrator. Adam enjoyed relationship with God in a perfect environment. Having bestowed Adam with free moral agency and the responsibility to rule, it was natural to prove Adam's faithfulness to God's will. The condition of this test is recorded in Genesis 2:16–17 in the form of a prohibition. Adam could eat from any tree in the garden, save for one: the Tree of the Knowledge of Good and Evil. The consequence for disobedience was broken relationship with God (spiritual death) which resulted in physical death.

Satan came to Eve in the form of a serpent (taking the physical form of a creature which Eve was responsible to subjugate to God's will) and deceived her into eating the fruit of the Tree of the Knowledge of Good and Evil. Adam, who was responsible for Eve, chose to eat with her, volitionally succumbing to rebellion against God. Adam broke his dependence on God's will and submitted himself to the will of Satan. In so doing, he both disobeyed God's specific instructions not to eat from the forbidden tree, and failed to rule over creation, having chosen to submit himself to the will of that which he had been responsible to govern: the serpent. As Dr. Woods notes in *The Coming Kingdom*:

> Instead of governing the physical world for God, Adam and Eve were influenced by creation (the serpent) to rebel against God (Gen. 3). Such rebellion represented a top to bottom reversal of God's original intention for the office of Theocratic Administrator... Satan's success in inciting this rebellion effectively removed the office of Theocratic Administrator from the earth, as Satan at that point became the ruler of the world.[16]

Satan became the *de facto* ruler of creation, not by receiving the right to rule, but by conquering the will of those to whom rulership belonged. He rules the earth because he rules the hearts of sinful and unregenerate mankind (Eph. 2:1–3). Elliot Johnson explains,

> Man's delegated right to rule on earth as stewards was lost to the serpent. The serpent now ruled Adam and the woman in their disobedience. While the image of God as a person remained (Gen 9:6), their self-awareness radically changed. They no longer saw themselves as stewards of God, but rather as enemies of God. And as enemies, their determination was to be like God themselves. Mankind had become alienated from God. Their minds were darkened and their wills driven by the serpent's lie.[17]

Chafer notes regarding the purpose and career of Satan that,

> Satan's purpose did not consist merely of rejecting God; he was designing a vast cosmos world system in which he proposed to utilize and misappropriate the elements which belong to God's creation, which, in themselves, are good.

---

[16] Andrew Woods, *The Coming Kingdom: What Is the Kingdom and How is Kingdom Now Theology Changing the Focus of the Church?* (Duluth, MN: Grace Gospel Press, 2016), 8-9.

[17] Elliot Johnson, *A Dispensational Biblical Theology,* (Allen, TX: Bold Grace Ministries, 2016), 58.

> Satan creates nothing. No step in the satanic cosmos project was more essential than that he should secure the allegiance of humanity. The issues at stake in the Garden of Eden were, in respect to Satan's career, such as would determine his realization of his whole undertaking. He must gain supremacy over man or fail completely. Little did Adam and Eve realize that, so far from attaining independence, they were becoming bondslaves to sin and Satan.[18]

Satan sought to establish his own will over God's mediatorial kingdom. Being unable to create, he could only hope to corrupt; he had to subject man's will to his own, as it had been designed to reflect God's will on earth. This he did, and as he ruled over man's hearts, he ruled over their domain and became like a god to this world (2 Cor. 4:4; Jn. 12:31; 1 Jn. 5:19). But Satan has never been fooled into considering the domain of man's hearts to be the kingdom which he seeks; that would only come in a literal, physical kingdom on earth.[19] Nevertheless, he has convinced many Bible students to accept Jesus' non-physical rule over the hearts of man as the fulfillment of God's kingdom program.

Satan does not envy our position as God's mediators between creation and Creator; he envies God the Creator. In his corrupt logic, if he usurps the kingdom through the mediators, he will take the place of God. Satan is not content to *rule in the hearts of men* as he does today (Eph. 2:1–2; Col. 1:13).

Satan will, in the end, attempt to put his own *man* on the throne of his *cosmos* world system so that through his satanic mediatorial king he might play god over the earth. His high position in God's creation, as God's anointed cherub on His holy mountain (Ezek. 28:14) has deluded him as to his own power. "Your heart was lifted up because of your beauty; You corrupted your wisdom by reason of your splendor

---

[18] Lewis Sperry Chafer, *Systematic Theology,* vol. 2, (Dallas, TX: Dallas Seminary Press, 1947), 250.

[19] Satan's demonic manifesto is found in Isaiah 14:12-14.

(Ezek. 28:17a)." It is unnecessary to wonder how Satan thinks he will succeed in usurping God's throne; he has blinded himself and has corrupted his wisdom. Cunning he has, wisdom he has not. Savvy he is, rational he is not.

When sin entered the world, man and creation became irreparably damaged by the sinfulness of rebellion against God's will. God intervened in the form of a curse (judgment) and a promise (salvation). Genesis 3:14–19 records God's judgment and plan to save His creation. Judgment was handed down from God to the serpent, to Eve, and to Adam. However, the judgment of the serpent doubled as a promise to mankind of a coming "seed" which would "crush the head of the serpent (Gen. 3:15)." In this way, God promised his fallen mediators a savior who would restore God's kingdom to earth.

A *New Civilization*

Peter's divine interpretation of Noah's flood and the judgment to come preserves excellent insight into one of God's means of forestalling the predations of *cosmos* rule while he works to fulfill His purposes in this creation. Second Peter 3:5b–7, 10, 13 states,

> …by the word of God the heavens existed long ago and the earth was formed out of water and by water, through which *the world at that time [ante-diluvian civilization]* was destroyed, being flooded with water. But by His word *the present heavens and earth [post-diluvian civilization]* are being reserved for fire, kept for the day of judgment and destruction of ungodly men… But the day of the Lord will come like a thief, in which the heavens will pass away with a roar and the elements will be destroyed with intense heat, and the earth and its works will be burned up… But according to His promise we are looking for *new heavens and a new earth [Messianic civilization]*, in which righteousness dwells *(emphasis and notations added).*

Peter speaks of three different worlds: *the world at that time* which was destroyed by the flood; *the present heavens and earth* which will be destroyed by fire, and *new heavens and a new earth* which will be characterized by righteousness (Isa. 28:17). Peter's three worlds are the Ante-Diluvian Civilization[20] (from Adam to the Flood), the Post-Diluvian Civilization (from the Flood to the end of the Great Tribulation), and the Messianic Kingdom Civilization, from the time of Jesus' return at the end of the Great Tribulation with the duration of one thousand years (Rev. 20). These civilizations of world history—past, present, and future—have served to progress God's restoration of creation through the Seed promise.

In Noah's day, mankind had become hopelessly corrupt (Gen. 6:12). Humankind was threatened with angelic interbreeding, risking not only the Seed promise of a human redeemer, but also the creation purpose of a human ruler. The interbreeding created a slew of half-breeds called Nephilim (Gen. 6:4), one of Satan's means of corrupting God's creation into his own corruption of the mediatorial kingdom: the cosmos system. The result of this sin was damaging enough to warrant the complete destruction of the world.

Protective Institution: Government

When God had destroyed the Ante-Diluvian *world at that time* with the Flood and carried eight humans through the destruction, He planted them in the *present heavens and earth* and re-established His purpose for them to rule over creation on his behalf. He installed a new absolute social structure into this new civilization to protect humanity while God prepared the world for His kingdom. He began by delegating the prerogative to protect human life from the predations of rebellion against God's righteousness. This provision came in the form of the divine institution of civil government. Its primary tool for curbing evil would be capital punishment. Wielded responsibly, this tool would give the government authority and ability to preserve mankind (Gen. 9:1–7) against the destructive results of

[20] The term "civilization" is used here to mean "periods of human history that begin with believers only, then populate and progress to a state of maximum degeneracy, and finally end with a divine judgment that removes all unbelievers from the earth," as it is defined in R. B. Thieme Jr., *Thieme's Bible Doctrine Dictionary*, (Houston, TX: R. B. Thieme, Jr., Bible Ministries, 2022), 39.

sin.[21] The present civilization is occupied with establishing a throne for God's chosen king and in carving out a people for His kingdom.

Preservative Institution: Nations

God's institution of human government was quickly co-opted by Satan, who placed his own man, Nimrod (whose name means rebellion), on the throne of a kingdom with a mediatorial rule over all the earth, and even sought, as Satan does, to establish its throne in the heavens (Gen. 11:4). God would not allow Satan to have his way. He dissolved the government of Nimrod by confusing the languages of the world so that evil could not feign unity through the use of language. In this way, God perforated the social fabric of humanity by creating another protective institution: the nation-state. God would preserve the present civilization from reaching the level of corruption that the Ante-Diluvian civilization had until the final civilization is prepared for God's chosen king.

God divided the languages and family-states of mankind to restrict the world's ability to communicate effectively and promote the will of Satan in mankind's rule over creation. While blocking the cosmic throne of Satan from formulating in Babel, God began His work of procuring a people for the purpose of establishing His own king and kingdom over creation. He did this by preserving His revealed will in written form and a people through whom the ruler to enact that will would come: the nation of Israel.

God demonstrated His genius in His ability to deal with these nations individually rather than globally in the Sodom and Gomorrah event. In this civilization, God can destroy a corrupt nation without destroying the whole earth as He did in the flood. The nation-state protects the world from premature global judgment, but it also laid the necessary framework for God's theocratic rule over the mediatorial kingdom. It was through the institution of civil government and national and linguistic isolation that He carved out a peculiar people

---

[21] Civil government is a positive creation necessary for bringing about theocratic government. Jesus will rule over the world in this form of government first instituted by God to Noah (Isa. 9:6–7; 65:20; Zech. 14:17–19; Rev. 20:7–9).

and a single nation to serve as a microcosm of creation—God will first place His king over the creation of Israel before He places Israel over all the nations, and her king over all creation.

Abrahamic Covenant

God's promise of a savior Seed is expanded through His covenant with Abraham and the subsequent sub-covenants with Israel. The first eleven chapters of Genesis record the continued failures of humanity to submit to God and demonstrate faithful obedience. After the rebellious actions of Nimrod at Babel, God choose to pursue the earthly kingdom through a single family. God chose Abraham, called him out of his homeland, and promised him a large swath of land, literal and earthly,[22] as an inheritance. God's initial promise to Abraham is recorded in Genesis 12:2–3:

> And I will make you a great nation,
> And I will bless you,
> And make your name great;
> And so you shall be a blessing;[23]
> And I will bless those who bless you,
> And the one who curses you I will curse.
> And in you all the families of the earth will be blessed.

God reaffirmed His promise to Abraham in Genesis 13:14–18. Chapter 14 records a significant event, which sees Abraham blessing his neighbor, Bera, King of Sodom, through military aid against an

---

[22] The literal nature of these promises are clear in scripture. The dimensions of the land have specific borders (Gen. 15:18); the land was physically inhabited (12:6; 13:7; 15:19–21); God instructed Abraham to walk through the land, requiring physical space (13:17), etc. Therefore, this promised land must be literal and earthly, just as the promised kingdom will be literal and physical and earthly.

[23] It should be noted that the predicate of "you shall be a blessing" is imperatival, not simple future. Abram was instructed to mete out God's blessings among his neighbors upon entering the promised land.

aggressive eastern confederate army.[24] Upon emerging victorious, Abraham meets Melchizedek, who is both a king and a priest. As a priest, Melchizedek mediates between sinful man and perfect God; as a king, Melchizedek exercises mediation over a subsection of God's creation. The respective offices of king and priest will maintain strict distinction in the nation of Israel but will find their unison again in God's ultimate Theocratic Administrator—One which both represents creation and humanity to God, and which represents God to creation. On this matter, John Philipps writes, "God's ideal priest is not a ritual priest after the order of Aaron, but a royal priest after the order of Melchizedek."[25]

Abraham refuses to take spoil from Bera. In doing so, Abraham "identifies with the kind of king-priest role that Melchizedek represents. Abram is thus adopting a king-priest role originally given to Adam and now given to him."[26] Abraham's encounter with Melchizedek is important in understanding the obedience of Abraham and what endeared him to God. Contrary to Adam who chose to submit his will to the will of a created and rebellious entity, Abraham sought God's will and glory. He acted as a conduit of blessing to his neighbors; rather than taking for himself the land which God had deeded to him, he blessed Lot, the kings and city-states of the Jordan Valley, his allies in Hebron, and even God Himself through His mediating priest, Melchizedek.

---

[24] One may see in this a foreshadow (but not a prediction) of the final battle when the kingdom of this world is finally wrested from the eastern confederate army of the False Messiah in the battle of Armageddon.

[25] John Phillips, *Exploring Genesis,* (Chicago, IL: Moody Press, 1980), 125.

[26] As Gentry notes, this king-priest role was first given to Adam and is seen in the king of Salem. Jesus Christ, seed of Abraham (Gal. 3:16), will be the second Adam, priest of Melchizedekian order, and seed of Abraham and the woman (Eve) who will rule over earth on God's behalf as the perfect Theocratic Administrator, retrieving rule over this world from Satan the usurper. Peter J. Gentry and Stephen J. Wellum, *God's Kingdom through God's Covenants: A Concise Biblical Theology* (Wheaton, IL: Crossway, 2015), 100–101.

Adam chose Satan's will for the cosmos system rather than the exercise of God's will over creation; Abraham chose God's will. God began to cultivate in Abraham the spiritual and ancestral line of the king who was to come. After all, it is not the priesthood of Levi which Jesus fulfills, but the priesthood of Melchizedek. Ross elaborates on the tie between Melchizedek and Jesus, the true heir to earth's throne:

> Preceding Abram, he was not a Levitical priest. When David, the first Israelite king to sit on Melchizedek's throne, prophesied that his great Descendant, the Messiah, would be a priest forever after the order of Melchizedek (Ps. 110:4), David looked beyond the Levitical priesthood which would be done away with. The Book of Hebrews demonstrates how Jesus Christ in His death fulfilled the Levitical order and began a better high priesthood.[27]

After the blessing by Melchizedek, Abraham had shown himself faithful where Adam had not, choosing the spiritual things of God over the earthly lusts of the flesh. God promised and assured Abraham of a great reward by establishing a legal contract, known as a covenant. The covenant which God made with Abraham is known to theologians as the Abrahamic Covenant. This required an elaborate ceremony in which sacrificial animals are divided in two and the parties to the covenant walk together between the severed animal corpses.[28]

The ceremony is performed in Genesis 15:17, but Abraham was in a deep sleep during its ratification (v. 12). The two parties which

---

[27] Allen P. Ross, "Genesis," in *The Bible Knowledge Commentary: An Exposition of the Scriptures*, ed. J. F. Walvoord and R. B. Zuck, vol. 1 (Wheaton, IL: Victor Books, 1985), 54.

[28] Gentry explains the implication of this oath: "The ceremony of covenant making involves an oath in which the covenant partners bring the curse of death upon themselves if they are not faithful to the covenant relationship and promises. Walking between the animals cut in half is a way of saying, "May I become like these dead animals if I do not keep my promise(s) and my oath." Scholars describe this as a self-maledictory oath, i.e., an oath where one brings the curse of death upon oneself for violating the covenant commitments." P. Gentry, 110.

passed through the animal corpses were both God: a smoking oven and a flaming torch.

Not only did God legally contract Himself to fulfill His promises to Abraham, but He also showed Himself to be intimately involved, not aloof or distant from the world. God fulfilled both party obligations to the covenant, and thus made the covenant unconditional for Abraham. Gentry elaborates: "The fact that only God passes between the pieces is quite remarkable and shows that the promise depends upon him and him alone."[29] It follows that all the promises given to Abraham will be fulfilled by God, and if God fails to produce His promises, He alone bears the consequences. The promises of the Abrahamic covenant are without human condition, predicated alone on the *I will* statements of God, about which Chafer says, "The phrase *I will* is, more than any other which language can exhibit, the sole prerogative and solemn right of Deity."[30] God alone can predict with such certainty the fulfillment of a promise, and for Him to be God, He must be able to produce this end despite the rebellious will of humanity.

The covenant with Abraham has been recognized as threefold, later expanded in three sub-covenants: the promised land (Gen. 15:18–21; expanded in the land covenant of Deut. 29-30), the promised seed (Gen. 15:4–5; expanded in the Davidic covenant of 2 Sam. 7:12–16 and 1 Chron. 17), and the promised blessing (Gen. 15:1; expanded in the prophets, see for example Jer. 31:31–34). God's purpose in Israel reflects His purpose in all of creation: for a man to rule in subjection to His will.

Each of the three aspects of the Abrahamic Covenant indicate ownership to the line of Abraham through Isaac and Jacob; however, ownership and enjoyment of these promises are not one in the same. A second covenant controls Israel's *enjoyment* of these Abrahamic promises. This covenant is the Mosaic Covenant, given to Israel through Moses after the Exodus in which God brought Israel out of

---

[29] P. Gentry, 111.

[30] Chafer, *Systematic Theology*, vol. 2, 246.

captivity in Egypt after growing them into a mighty and sizeable people, isolated from the influence of pagan culture.

Before we turn our focus to the Mosaic Covenant and the establishment of a theocratic government in Israel, we must first observe God's preparations for a king to rule over the nation of Israel. This prophecy comes via Jacob in the 49th chapter of Genesis, regarding his son, Judah.

> The scepter shall not depart from Judah,
> Nor the ruler's staff from between his feet,
> Until Shiloh comes,
> And to him shall be the obedience of the peoples (Gen. 49:10).

Just as the savior must be a human from the seed of Adam and Eve, and a descendant of Noah in his humanity, so the ruler over the nation of Israel who would one day serve as the ruler over God's creation must also be the Seed of Abraham and Sarah (Gen. 17:16), through the line of Judah.

Exodus 19:6 is the first time the term "kingdom" is used explicitly in scripture. God intended to restore theocratic rule to the mediatorial kingdom through the election of Israel as His chosen nation. He made it incumbent upon Israel to enthrone the king which God would choose for them (cf. Deut. 17:15). God governed through Moses, then Joshua, then the judges, and the first kings of Israel, but it was always the responsibility of Israel to recognize the coming of the promised seed and to install Him as their king.

The Mosaic Covenant

The Law is given in Exodus 20–40, and the book of Deuteronomy. The Law text is formatted like a Hittite Suzerain-vassal treaty, common to the Ancient Near East at the time of the Exodus.[31]

---

[31] Eugene H. Merrill, Mark F. Rooker, and Michael A. Grisanti, The Word and the World: An Introduction to the Old Testament, (Nashville, TN: B&H Publishing Group, 2011), 258-259.

This brings to light the nationalistic nature of a kingdom, in that its structure was understood contemporarily as a legal, national document, much like a constitution. A Suzerain-vassal treaty was drawn between a Suzerain (the dominant national leader) and a vassal (a subjugated national leader). The contract depended upon the faithful service of the vassal to the conditions of the Suzerain, and the Suzerain would fulfill his promised obligations to the vassal. As Gentry explains, the Mosaic covenant is similar to ancient Near Eastern *law-codes* in content, but like an ancient Near Eastern *covenant* in form. Gentry explains the importance of this:

> God desires to rule in the midst of his people as King. He wants to direct, guide, and instruct their lives and lifestyle. Yet he wants to do this in the context of a relationship of love, loyalty, and trust. This is completely different from Greek and Roman law codes or ancient Near Eastern law codes. They represent an impersonal code of conduct binding on all citizens and enforced by penalties from a controlling authority. We should always remember that Torah, by contrast, means personal "instruction" from God as Father and King of his people.[32]

God's intimate relationship with Israel is implicit throughout both the Abrahamic Covenant and the Mosaic Covenant. God intended to make Israel a nation through whom and among whom He would rule. Through the limited form of theocracy, God did rule in and among His people for a limited time and to a limited degree.

Covenant Conditionality

God instituted a theocracy under Moses. He again arranged to rule through man while dwelling among them, though in a single nation until it was time to elevate that nation to global supremacy. Through this theocratic government, God would one day restore theocratic rule to the mediatorial kingdom. The instructions given to Israel through Moses conditioned enjoyment of their national

---

[32] Gentry, 168.

promises.[33] The *if/then* format of these blessings makes their conditionality unequivocal. Three promises are given to Israel. If they listen to God's voice and keep His commandments, they will be God's people and His possession, a kingdom of priests, and a holy nation. The Law rests upon this *if/then* statement.

The Law of Moses was a rule of life for God's saved people, Israel. It allowed them to enjoy the land while God worked in them to bring about the seed and full blessing. Nevertheless, the generation to whom the Law was given—the generation which God brought out of Egypt—immediately failed to obey God's revealed will. Just as rebellion against God's will has spoiled many of man's experiences of God's creation mandate, so in Israel God prevents Israel from enjoying their possession because of rebellion. For this reason, they were barred from the promised land and made to wander the wilderness for forty years until their children could enter the land. But when the first generation was punished, the second generation was given a new opportunity to obey and enjoy God's covenant blessings. These events are recorded in the book of Numbers. Deuteronomy is the second giving of the Law to the generation which did enter the promised land.

When viewed side by side, it becomes apparent that the unconditionality of the Abrahamic Covenant, and the conditionality of the Mosaic Covenant do not readily harmonize. It is necessary to avoid blurring the lines between these covenants, and to let each one stand distinct, having diverse functions but working together for God's kingdom purpose in Israel. The Abrahamic Covenant gives Israel unconditional positional ownership of land, seed, and blessing promises. The Mosaic Covenant gives Israel realized (experiential) enjoyment of these promises. The Mosaic Covenant does not have

---

[33] Note the conditional language used in Exodus 19:5-6: "Now then, *if* you will indeed obey My voice and keep My covenant, *then* you shall be My own possession among all the peoples, for all the earth is Mine; and you shall be to Me a kingdom of priests and a holy nation.' These are the words that you shall speak to the sons of Israel."

within its domain the ability to override God's unconditional promises to Abraham.

God gave Abraham a gift which cannot be taken away. That gift belongs to Israel, and it will always be Israel's property. Israel's ownership of that gift passes on from generation to generation. While enjoyment of the land may not be experienced by all generations, such as the Exodus generation and the Exilic generations, it will be realized in part by some, and in full in the Messianic civilization.

Consider this illustration: The Abrahamic Covenant is like the title deed to a car. Israel owns this car, but without a valid driver's license, use of the car is not permissible. However, if Israel obtains a valid driver's license and obeys the traffic laws, Israel may enjoy the car which it legally owns. After obtaining this driver's license (the Mosaic Covenant), she may operate the car within the parameters of the law. Failure to follow the law may result in a suspended license. A suspended license does not mean ownership of the car has been lost, only that the owner has proven herself too irresponsible to enjoy the benefits of operating it at that time.

God tells Israel in essence, *when you get a ticket—and you will get many tickets—there will be certain increasing consequences.* They get ticket after ticket until eventually, the license is suspended. Now, that car sits in the garage waiting to be driven. They still own it, but they are not able to drive it. So is it with Israel's cycles of judgment under the Mosaic Law. They are legal owners of God's earthly theocracy which will one day enthrone Jesus the Messiah—God's ultimate Theocratic Administrator—but until they are faithful to the Mosaic Law by receiving the One who fulfilled the Law perfectly (Rom. 10:4), they will not receive enjoyment of all that belongs to them by inheritance.

The Law of Moses presumes the failure of Israel, while simultaneously prophesying the remedy for their failure. Deuteronomy chapters 27 and 28[34] lay out Israel's cycle of blessing and cursing. They

---

[34] Also see Leviticus 26 for Israel's anticipated failure over time seen in the first giving of the law to the first generation of Israel coming out of the Exodus.

will be faithful in some generations, and unfaithful in others, and so they will experience both blessing and cursing under the Mosaic Covenant. Nevertheless, ultimate victory is guaranteed, not through their faithfulness to God, but through God's faithfulness to them.

Since the penalties for disobedience in Deuteronomy had to do with enjoyment of the promised land, God saw fit to reinforce the unconditionality and expand the details of the Land Covenant through further progressive revelation between His warning of cyclic blessing and cursing and the promise of future restoration. Deuteronomy 29 records what has been known to prior generations as the Palestinian Covenant, but which has become known to modern generations as the Land Covenant. This name is derived from the content of the covenant. A section of land in the Levant was unconditionally granted to Israel by God, whose land it is to give, since this is to be the seat of His mediatorial throne on earth. In Deuteronomy 29, this covenant is referred to as the "the covenant which the Lord commanded Moses to make with the sons of Israel in the land of Moab (Dt. 29:1)." This geographical name distinguished the covenant from the Mosaic Covenant, which had been made in Horeb (Dt. 29:1).

In Deuteronomy 30, God promises to restore a future generation of Israel which has been scattered from the land of Israel because of covenant disobedience.

> So it shall be when all of these things have come upon you, the blessing and the curse which I have set before you, and you call them to mind in all nations where the Lord your God has banished you, and you return to the Lord your God and obey Him with all your heart and soul according to all that I command you today, you and your sons, then the Lord your God will restore you from captivity, and have compassion on you, and will gather you again from all the peoples where the Lord your God has scattered you (Deut. 30:1–3).

No matter what, the land belongs to Israel. Use of their land is contingent on their relationship with God as He has outlined the rule of life for Israel in the Law of Moses. The obedience of this passage pertains to their singular sin of rejecting the king whom God choose to rule over them in anticipation of the fulfillment of His kingdom purpose in and through the unique nation of Israel (cf. Lev. 26, Deut. 28). However, only the progress of revelation would reveal that one sin which would send Israel scattered across the globe.[35]

Theocratic Kingdom of Israel

Although Israel constantly fell into disbelief and disobedience, God was still working behind the scenes to move forward His kingdom preparations. First Samuel 8 records Israel's plea for a king like the kings of the surrounding nations. A king was always in the plan of God, but Israel was not willing to wait on the Lord for the king whom God had in store for them. In the end, they installed Saul as the first king of Israel. Saul proved to be a worldly king more like Bera of Sodom than Melchizedek of Salem. God dethroned Saul and put David on the throne—*a* king of God's choosing through whom *the* king of God's choosing would be born.

David was, unlike Saul, a man after God's own heart. He was passionate in His worship of God, and swift to repentance, and he was a descendant from the line of Judah (cf. Gen. 49:10; Rev. 5:5), where Saul was from the line of Benjamin. Under David, Israel prospered in many of the ways which the Abrahamic Covenant had promised. Nevertheless, the fullness of the covenant promises has yet to be experienced, and so await their fulfillment until a future time when

---

[35] It should also be noted that Israel's scattering was both a punishment as well as a preservative. No nation has ever retained its national identity while not functioning as a localized nation for such an extended period of time. God has miraculously kept the sons of Israel distinct for His purposes while perforating their nation just as he had perforated the nations at Babel. To keep Israel from being destroyed completely, God scattered them until He is ready to bring them back together for the final generation to receive their king. Israel serves as a microcosm of God's purposes on earth. In fulfilling his purpose to have a king of His choosing rule over the land of Israel, he will expand His rule to include all of creation and fulfill his purpose for earth. The very continuance of this creation is appropriately united with God's perseverance toward Israel (Jer. 31:36).

national Israel will experience the full blessing of the Abrahamic covenant under king Jesus.

David's love for God is evident in Second Samuel 7. David sought to build a house for the Lord, and the Lord in response made a covenant with David. "When your days are complete and you lie down with your fathers, I will raise up your descendant after you, who will come forth from you, and I will establish his kingdom. He shall build a house for My name, and I will establish the throne of his kingdom forever (2 Sam. 7:12–13)."

First Chronicles 17 records the same covenant between God and the house of David, only this record makes it clear that Solomon is not the fulfillment of the promise; he is only the type of that fulfillment. First Chronicles 17:11–14 records,

> When your days are fulfilled that you must go to be with your fathers ... I will set up one of your descendants after you, who will be of your sons; and I will establish his kingdom. He shall build for Me a house, and I will establish his throne forever. I will be his father and he shall be My son; and I will not take My lovingkindness away from him, as I took it from him who was before you. But I will settle him in My house and in My kingdom forever, and his throne shall be established forever.

First Chronicles promises that the descendant (lit. seed) of David would be established forever over the eternal house of David, on his eternal throne in his eternal kingdom being an eternal descendant. This cannot speak of Solomon, nor the Solomonic empire which divided after Solomon's death (1 Ki. 11:31–35). Second Samuel 7 promises that God will be a Father to David's immediate descendant (Solomon), chastising him when he commits iniquity; 1 Chronicles 17 promises that God will be the Father to David's future descendant, without reference to any sin or chastisement, because David's ultimate descendant would be the God-man Jesus, the second Adam, who proves Himself faithful to God in all things, sinless—without a sin nature and without rebellion against God's will—and so worthy to be the king over God's creation.

Just as man had failed globally between the Fall at Eden and the Dispersion at Babel, so national Israel failed under the Law, as predicted in Deuteronomy 29. Eventually, disobedience persisted to such a degree that the kingdom of Israel was divided into the northern tribes of Israel and the southern tribes of Judah and Benjamin. Idolatry had profaned the people and the land. Evil was rampant in Israel. The judgments of the Mosaic Law detailed in Deuteronomy 28 went into effect. First the northern tribes were taken into captivity by the Assyrians in 722 B.C.; then, Judah was taken into captivity in 586 B.C. by Babylon.

Just as God's manifest presence—His Shekinah glory—had been localized in Eden, the place of God's meeting with His people, so His glory had been the unique boast of Israel, residing in the temple in the Holy of Holies. His glory had come to rest where His rule over creation would one day be manifested. Unbeknownst to Israel, that very glory which had filled the temple would one day bleed and die to pay for the sins of the world, before being glorified to rule over creation as God's Mediatorial King. Before he did, however, his physical presence departed from Israel while Israel underwent the predicted chastisement for failure under the Mosaic Law. While the Shekinah glory was not present in Israel, mediatorial rule over creation passed through various Gentile administrators. This became known as the time of the Gentiles (Lk. 21:24), until such a time as Israel was ready to receive the king of God's choosing.

Old Testament Prophets and the Exile

Ezekiel, a Jewish prophet, witnessed the Shekinah glory of God departing the Temple in Jerusalem (Ezek. 10:18–19). The departure of the glory signaled the end of the theocracy in Israel when God ruled among His people from within the Holy of Holies by a human administrator. The glory will return to the Millennial Temple when Jesus rules on earth as the Theocratic Administrator over God's Mediatorial Kingdom (Ezek. 43:4–5). The time of the Gentiles spans the period of the glory's departure and the glory's return in the Messianic kingdom. Daniel gives a more complete outline of the time of the Gentiles in the form of two prophetic visions.

While in Babylon, the Lord used Daniel providentially to interpret a dream given to Nebuchadnezzar. The second chapter of Daniel records this dream. It outlines five kingdoms which would exercise mediatorial power over earth during the Time of the Gentiles. The kingdoms were represented in the form of a magnificent statue of five distinct materials. Its head was gold, its breast and arms silver, its belly and thighs bronze, its legs iron, and its feet a mixture of iron and clay. A large stone[36] which struck the feet of iron and clay, crushing them, and the stone grew into a mountain, representing a sixth kingdom which would replace the Gentile reign over the earth to supplant it with the heavenly (Dan. 2:44) kingdom of God.

God revealed this dream to Daniel, who interpreted it for Nebuchadnezzar. The first element of the statue, the head of gold, was Babylon, with Nebuchadnezzar as its ruler. The second, the breast and arms of silver, was Medo-Persia, which overthrew king Darius, the nephew of Nebuchadnezzar. The next kingdom, the bronze belly, was Greece. Greece ruled in the centuries prior to Christ, introducing the Greek language and Hellenizing much of the Mediterranean. The final kingdom, the iron legs, was Rome, which overthrew the Greeks and ruled over Jerusalem during the time of Christ. This empire was never conquered; rather, its power dwindled and grew into the conglomerate of today's Western powers. The legs, not being conquered, merge into the feet of iron and clay, which are yet to come.

The feet of iron and clay are part of the fourth kingdom of Rome but will materialize under the authority of a false Messiah who will attempt to usurp the mediatorial throne by establishing the cosmos kingdom under Satan's power (Rev. 13:2). Externally, he will have the

---

[36] This stone is notably cut without the use of human tools, indicating that it is not fashioned by humans as the statue was, but by God alone. It is hard for the church to argue that it is the duty of the church to establish God's kingdom on earth as it will not be made with human hands.

crushing strength of iron but internally the fragility of clay. His kingdom will contain ten smaller fiefs but will eventually be destroyed by the "stone cut without hands" which is the true Messiah of God, whose theocratic kingdom will grow to fill the earth.

In Daniel chapter seven, Daniel was given a vision of four terrible beasts. "These great beasts, which are four in number, are four kings who will arise from the earth. But the saints of the Highest One will receive the kingdom and possess the kingdom forever, for all ages to come (Dan. 7:17–18)." These four beasts that came out of the sea were the gentile nations that would dominate Israel until the return of the theocracy. The first beast was like a lion with eagle wings; its wings were torn off, and it was made to stand and think like a human. This beast is the same as the head of gold in Nebuchadnezzar's vision, namely, Babylon. The second beast, a bear, lifted on one side, had three ribs in its mouth and it was told to "devour much meat." This was Medo-Persia. The third beast was a leopard with four wings and four heads. This was Greece. The last of the beasts was said to be "dreadful and terrifying and extremely strong (Dan. 7:7)."

This fourth beast had large iron teeth, and it devoured and crushed and trampled with its feet. Daniel noted that it was different from the other three beasts. Just as the feet of Nebuchadnezzar's dreams grew out of the legs of iron, so horns grow out of the head of Daniel's fourth beast. Among those horns a little horn grew, and three of the original horns were pulled out by the roots. The little horn had eyes and a mouth, and it said blasphemous things. In the vision, Daniel watched the "Ancient of Days" destroy the blaspheming beast and burn it, utterly destroying the fourth beast.

Nebuchadnezzar's dream comes from the perspective of the conqueror, and Daniel's vision from the conquered. The first was an image of might, because it was a dominating power over Israel; yet, Daniel's vision was of hideous beasts, because they represented the oppressors of Daniel's Jewish brethren. Both Nebuchadnezzar's dream and Daniel's vision represent the same period of Gentile domination which will last until the Messianic kingdom replaces Gentile rule over creation. This is seen in Ezekiel 43 with the re-entry of the divine presence into the temple.

Daniel's 70 Weeks

Daniel, being both a prophet and a student of God's past prophets, knew from Jeremiah's prophecies that the captivity in Babylon would last only 70 years. He also knew from the Law, in Deuteronomy 30:1–10 and Leviticus 26:40–45, that Israel would experience captivity in a foreign land before God would fulfill His covenant program and ushered in the kingdom. As Leviticus 26:40–42 stipulates, this would be precipitated by the national repentance of Israel for their sin *[singular]* and the sin of their forefathers. Thus, Daniel, at the end of 70 years in captivity, began to confess the sins of Israel (Dan. 9:1–19). And although he correctly interpreted Leviticus 26 and Deuteronomy 30 as prophetic passages, he mistakenly applied them to his own day. God sent Gabriel to correct Daniel's understanding of the kingdom program. The angel told Daniel that the kingdom would not manifest to Israel at the end of the 70 years in Babylonian captivity, but rather after 70 *weeks* of years.[37] Daniel would have to wait 490 years to see the kingdom program fulfilled. Of course, Daniel would not live that long in his pre-glory body (Dan. 12:13).

Six things remain as pre-requisites for the beginning of the kingdom, and they will not be complete until the 70 weeks of years are complete. These are detailed in Daniel 9:24.

> "Seventy weeks have been decreed for your people and your holy city, (1) to finish the transgression, (2) to make an

[37] This notion of "weeks" has long been a topic of discussion among those who study eschatology and those who try to attack it. It becomes, however, stunningly clear, in one realizes what Daniel was trying to accomplish in his prayer—namely the national confession of Israel to usher in the kingdom—that the angel's use of "weeks" was not simply a linguistic flourish of prophetic language, but rather a means of correcting Daniel's thinking by modifying his own delineation of time. Daniel expected 70 years; the angel multiplied his seventy-year expectation by seven (a week).

> end of sin, (3) to make atonement for iniquity, (4) to bring in everlasting righteousness, (5) to seal up vision and prophecy and (6) to anoint the most holy *place*.

The transgression (Lev. 26:40 cf. Dan. 9:24a) for which Daniel thought he was praying had not yet occurred. The commission of this sin will be discussed in the section on Israel's rejection of the kingdom offer. The second, third, and fourth pre-requisites for the kingdom look forward to the accomplishments of Jesus in His death and resurrection: to make an end of sin (ending the Mosaic law and bringing in the New) which was accomplished through His provision of unlimited atonement and imputed righteousness. The fifth looks forward not only to the fulfillment of God's revelation through the prophets, but to the finishing of that prophetic program. The cap of this program will be the beginning of the Messianic kingdom itself, the anointing of the Holy One,[38] which appears to correlate with the anointing of the King of Israel (Deut. 17:15).

God responded to Daniel's faith concerning the specificity and anticipation of prophetic fulfillment by revealing to him the most specific timeline in all of scripture concerning the inauguration of the kingdom. This is found in Daniel 9:25–27.

> 25 So you are to know and discern *that* from the issuing of a
> decree to restore and rebuild Jerusalem until Messiah the
> Prince *there will be* seven weeks and sixty-two weeks; it will
> be built again, with plaza and moat, even in times of
> distress. 26 Then after the sixty-two weeks the Messiah will
> be cut off and have nothing, and the people of the prince
> who is to come will destroy the city and the sanctuary. And
> its end *will come* with a flood; even to the end there will be
> war; desolations are determined. 27 And he will make a firm
> covenant with the many for one week, but in the middle of

---

[38] Although the NASB and many interpreters (cf. Gaebelein, Walvoord, Fruchtenbaum) see "the holy holy" at the end of verse 24 to be the consecrating of the Messianic temple, the Tribulation temple is referred to by the term "sanctuary" rather than "holy of holies" or "holy place" in verse 26.

> the week he will put a stop to sacrifice and grain offering; and on the wing of abominations *will come* one who makes desolate, even until a complete destruction, one that is decreed, is poured out on the one who makes desolate.

Israel would return to their land and rebuild the city and the temple under persecution from surrounding Gentile factions. This was the first seven of the 70 weeks of years prophesied. Once the temple was complete, a period of 62 weeks would follow "until Messiah the Prince."[39] Two things ought to be noted about this anticipated Messiah-Prince. First, he will be cut off and have nothing. This looks forward to the commission of Israel's great sin: the rejection of the Messiah. Secondly, he is called Prince, identifying him in his royal office in conjunction with the rebuilding of the city of Jerusalem. It may be seen as significant that he is cut off as a prince before he is anointed as king. He is a king-in-waiting until the conclusion of the 70 weeks of years.

Finally, verses 26b–27 explain what will occur after the Messiah is cut off. First, the same people who cut him off will be responsible for producing the final challenger the mediatorial throne: the False Messiah. He is "the prince who is to come" whose people will "destroy the city and the sanctuary." This refers to the destruction of the city and sanctuary which would be rebuilt after the return from Babylonian captivity, thus it was revealed to Daniel that not only was the kingdom not about the materialize, but even the temple and city which would be rebuilt would not last until the kingdom but would be destroyed by a rival to the Messiah. This same rival would initiate a covenant, but unlike the God of Israel and His Messiah, this false Messiah would not be a covenant keeper, but a covenant breaker. He would break the

---

[39] There is great debate over this timeline, even among conservative theologians and within Dispensationalism itself. The purpose of this paper is to view the theological significance of this prophecy in light of the kingdom, not to solve the historical problem of dating these events. For a comprehensive argument on this subject, see Arnold Fruchtenbaum, *The Book of Daniel: Exposition from a Messianic Jewish Perspective,* (San Antonio, TX: Ariel Ministries, 2023) and Dr. Daniel Woodhead's article entitled "The Houses of God" in this issue of Truth & Grace.

covenant of peace and persecute Israel, putting an end to their religious exercises in the temple, and even desecrate the temple in the process. But that kingdom too would be destroyed. This would all happen before the coming of the kingdom. Taken together with the two prophecies of the times of the Gentiles in Daniel 2 and 7, this prophecy would function as the most complete and specific prophecy on God's timeline for the kingdom program, and a warning to Israel about their future unfaithfulness.

The New Covenant

The hope of the prophets was for a physical and earthly kingdom where the Lord would rule over Israel and there would be peace in all the earth, not only in Israel (Isa. 9:6–7; Psa. 47). The prophets served as God's mouthpiece to Israel, reminding the nation of its covenant responsibilities. As the Mosaic covenant was distinctly a legal document, it was not only appropriate, but necessary for God to use the prophets as His *prosecuting attorneys*. In this way, the record of the prophets was often one of warning. Nevertheless, God's faithfulness stands in stark contrast to Israel's unfaithfulness in the messages of the prophets. Although Israel will not uphold her end of the contract, God will remain faithful to Israel and establish His kingdom on earth.

Though certain generations incurred the judgments outlined in the Mosaic covenant, God would yet establish His kingdom through Israel and bless the world through them. Prophecy and the prophets were necessary in times of judgment to remind Israel of the purpose of her judgment, but moreover, to bring to remembrance the promise of the anticipated perfect rule of Messiah.

The prophets of the Old Testament revealed much of what we know about God's plans for the coming earthly kingdom. However, the prophetic perspective notably looks over intervening periods of time, often not revealing interim events, so that certain fulfillments of prophecy do not immediately occur as they may appear when first delivered. An unseen gap of time often exists between correlated events. Larkin analogized this phenomenon as valleys which lay between mountain peaks:

> The Old Testament prophets spoke as they were moved by the Holy Spirit (2 Pet. 1:19–21). They did not understand what they prophesied (1 Pet. 1:10–12). They believed that their prophecies as to Christ were all to be fulfilled at his "First Coming". This accounts for why the people of Christ's Day looked for him to set up a "Temporal Kingdom". They did not see that this dispensation was to intervene between the "Cross," (The Suffering of Christ), and the "Crown" (The glory that should follow) (1 Pet. 1:11). The prophets saw the events they foretold as separate peaks of one great mountain.[40]

An example of this is Isaiah 9:6–7:

> For a child will be born to us, a son will be given to us;
> And the government will rest on His shoulders;
> And His name will be called Wonderful Counselor, Mighty God,
> Eternal Father, Prince of Peace.
> There will be no end to the increase of His government or of peace,
> On the throne of David and over his kingdom,
> To establish it and to uphold it with justice and righteousness
> From then on and forevermore.
> The zeal of the Lord of hosts will accomplish this.

The first line of this prophecy relates to the first coming of Christ, while the remainder pertains only to His second coming. Yet this appeared as a single prophetic event to Isaiah (cf. 1 Pet. 1:10–11). So important is the king to the kingdom that His entrance into the earth is rightly viewed alongside His eventual earthly reign. And so, it is important to consider the audience and purpose of this prophecy; Isaiah wrote to encourage the Exilic generation of Israel during their

---

[40] Clarence Larkin, *Dispensational Truth, or "God's Plan and Purpose in the Ages"*, (Philadelphia, PA: Clarence Larkin, 1918), *Chart*: The Mountain Peaks of Prophecy. Language and orthography updated for readability.

period of cursing under the Mosaic Covenant. The king will come and, the government will be upon His shoulders (Isa. 9:6) and He will rule with a rod of iron (Psa. 2:9; Rev. 12:5).[41]

God used various nations such as Babylon and Assyria to castigate Israel for her disobedience to the Mosaic covenant, since the Mosaic covenant would prepare them to receive the King of Righteousness who alone could keep the Law perfectly. Their global scattering, as opposed to the warning shocks of Assyrian and Babylonian captivity, would come from the ultimate breaking of the Law: rejecting the One who was the goal and end of the law (Rom. 10:4). Without receiving the king of God's choosing who engenders within Himself the righteousness of God through the Law, Israel cannot enjoy her covenant blessings.

However, the prophets were not only *prosecuting attorneys* calling Israel back to covenant faithfulness, but also God's mouthpiece for hope and security in the promises of God. Since God's promises to Israel in the Abrahamic covenant were eternal and irrevocable, God would fulfill his covenant with Israel to give them the land promised to Abraham, an eternal king, and the blessing of divine fellowship. A significant means of delivering hope to His people in captivity was to elaborate on *how* he would deliver on His promises. Just as He had elaborated on the land promise with the Land covenant when it was time for Israel to return to the promised land after captivity in Egypt, and just as He had elaborate on the seed promise with the Davidic covenant while King David was on the throne, so now while Israel was

---

[41] More than just an eternal, earthly kingdom, ruled by the seed of David, the prophets detailed many specific conditions of the coming Theocratic Kingdom. Andy Woods lists many of these promises in his book, *The Coming Kingdom*, including, but not limited to, the temple of Ezekiel 40-46; a kingdom characterized by righteousness (Is. 9:6–7); a new covenant (Jer. 31:31); the curse removed (Is. 65:20–22); universal peace (Is. 2:4); global agricultural prosperity (Amos 9:13–14); and many geographical/topographical changes. None of these kingdom conditions have ever been fulfilled and so must be fulfilled at some point in the future. Woods, *The Coming Kingdom*, 36-51, and Arnold Fruchtenbaum, *Israelology: The Missing Link in Systematic Theology*, revised 2020 ed., (San Antonio, TX: Ariel Ministries, 1989), 741–752.

in captivity in Babylon and Assyria, God elaborated on the blessing aspect of the Abrahamic covenant, telling Israel how he would bring about their experience of covenant blessings.

Unlike the Mosaic covenant which had been implemented to regulate blessing *and* cursing, depending on Israel's obedience to God's revealed will, the New Covenant would replace the Mosaic covenant and provide only blessing (Jer. 31:31–34). It had become clear that Israel, full of sinful humans, could not keep the perfect righteousness of God. The law itself had no ability whatever to help people keep the righteousness of God, only to condemn them for imperfection (Gal. 3:19–22). God's promise to Israel in the New Covenant was that He would cause them to be perfectly obedient, not through law, but through grace. In the New Covenant, God promised regeneration to Israel.

The fact remained, however, that the Law cannot simply pass out of existence; it must be fulfilled (Matt. 5:17–20). God would provide for both the fulfillment of the Mosaic Covenant and the establishment of the New in His Son, Jesus, Israel's Messiah, the Savior of the world, and the ultimate Mediator between God and man—the King of God's choosing.

The Mediatorial Kingdom in the New Testament

For four hundred years, God's prophets were silent in Israel. During this time, the world was prepared for the advent of the promised king who would fulfill the Old Testament expectation. As prophesied by Daniel, Babylon had fallen to Medo-Persia, and Medo-Persia to Greece, and Greece to Rome. Jerusalem was in the hands of the first form of the final Gentile kingdom, and the time had come for the true king to be born in Israel.

The King Incarnate

From the beginning of creation, God intended for humanity to rule over creation (Gen. 1:26–28). The record of history contained in the Old Testament is a divine commentary meant to demonstrate to humanity God's integrity and mankind's dependence upon Him. Time and time again the history and scripture reveal that man does not have the righteousness necessary to submit himself to the will of God and act in perfect obedience. Reading through the Old Testament, one might, like John in the heavenly throne room of Revelation 5, lament as no man is found worthy to take up the title deed to this earth and vindicate God's creation purpose.

God's solution to this deficit in humanity was the incarnation of His own Son. The significance of the incarnation of Jesus the Messiah cannot be underestimated while considering the program of the kingdom. The kingdom requires a righteous, eternal, and human king. Apart from God taking on the flesh of man Himself, such a combination is impossible. The incarnation is also the foundational truth which allows Jesus to die for our sins, however we must also recognize that the purpose of the incarnation goes beyond making Jesus suitable as a substitute for the salvation of mankind. It becomes the very means by which God fulfills His purpose for creation, to place a human over the mediatorial kingdom of creation to rule in perfect subjection to the will of God. Jesus is fully human and fully God, and he is the only one who can fulfill God's purpose for creation.

While the atonement became necessary after sin entered creation, and the incarnation was God's means of providing that atonement, it goes too far to constrain the purpose of the incarnation to atonement. Even without the atonement being made necessary through sin, it was the eternal purpose of God to glorify Himself through the incarnation with His Son as the ultimate Theocratic Administrator, heir to creation. Mankind was created in God's image in unconfirmed and finite holiness not only to reflect God's image. Mankind was made in God's image because His Son is "the radiance of His glory and the exact representation of His nature (Heb. 1:3)." Indeed, "He is the image of the invisible God, the firstborn [i.e., heir] of all creation (Col. 1:15)." Jesus was predestined to be glorified over all creation in the office of Theocratic Administrator, and we were made like Him in order that He might be made like us.

The Kingdom Offer

The prophets had predicted a forerunner who would precede the Messiah and prepare the way for His message (Isa. 40:3–5; Mal. 3:1). That forerunner was Jesus' cousin, John (Jn. 1:22–23). John preached the gospel of the kingdom to Israel, who would interpret this kingdom as the fulfillment of the Old Testament prophets.

The prophets of the Old Testament preached a message of repentance and covenant faithfulness to receive the blessings of the kingdom. As R. T. France notes in his commentary on Matthew, the term *repent* echoes the Old Testament prophets who called Israel back to covenant repentance.[42] The message of the Old Testament prophets was identical to John's message. John was aligning himself with the message of the kingdom as it had been prophesied by the Old Testament prophets, and in so doing, prepared the way for the king of God's choosing, Jesus Messiah.

The call to repent was for Israel only, and it was combined with the offer of the kingdom because first century Israel had abandoned the Mosaic Law and had replaced it with their rabbinic interpretations and traditions, elevating rabbinic Oral Law over the text of the Mosaic Law. The Mosaic Law had been written to show them their inability to perform the requirements of God's perfect righteousness, and to provoke them to look for the Messiah who could keep God's righteousness. Instead, they stripped the Law of its power by taking from it the righteousness of God and creating a wicked burden through works righteousness. Israel was to repent of this rejection of God's word so that they could see the perfect righteousness of God in Jesus the Messiah.

---

[42] Unfortunately, France misses the clear implication, reinterpreting this in terms of a soteriological and ecclesiological call to repentance, stating, "This radical conversion is necessary in the light of the coming of the kingdom of heaven… which here means the establishment of God's rightful sovereignty in judgment and in salvation, i.e. the Messianic age." R. T. France, *Matthew: An Introduction and Commentary*, vol. 1, Tyndale New Testament Commentaries (Downers Grove, IL: InterVarsity Press, 1985), 95–96.

The genealogy in the first chapter of Matthew establishes Jesus as the heir of the throne through David but apart from Jeconiah by means of the virgin birth; and the genealogy in Luke, likewise, shows that he is a man from the seed of Eve through Adam and an heir to the Davidic throne through Mary's line and David's son Nathan.

If Israel is to be faithful to their covenant with God, she must enthrone Jesus as her king (Dt. 17:15). If Israel were to enthrone Jesus—the second Adam and the son of David—theocracy would be restored to Israel and Jesus would retrieve rulership over the mediatorial kingdom from the Gentile powers. But Jesus did not offer the kingdom until after He proved Himself faithful where Adam (and all other potential administrators) had been unfaithful.

Jesus' life on earth shows one of obedience to God. Adam and Israel had been unfaithful to the words of God (His revealed will), and instead were overcome by, and even worshipped, the creation. On the other hand, Jesus showed Himself faithful, just as Abraham had been in the presence of Melchizedek. Jesus was tempted in all the ways Adam had been, and yet He showed that He was faithful to the revealed will of God. Each of the synoptic gospels include the account of Jesus' temptation in the wilderness. Larkin explains the temptation of Jesus this way:

> We are told that Jesus was "tempted in 'all points' like as we are, yet without sin." Heb. 4:15. These "all points" may be summed up under three heads, represented by the "Three Temptations" of Jesus, and were included in the "One Temptation" of Eve—(1) "The Lust of the flesh;" (2) "The Pride of Life," and (3) "The Lust of the eyes." 1 John 2:16. All the temptations of mankind may be summed up under three heads, represented by the Wilderness Temptations.[43]

---

[43] Clarence Larkin, Rightly Dividing the Word (Philadelphia, PA: Clarence Larkin, 1921), 171–172. Orthography altered for modern conventional usage.

Jesus faithfully overcame these temptations by operating in dependence upon God's word and His covenant promises. The devil offers Jesus bodily comfort, fame (a name for Himself), and finally, "all the kingdoms of the earth" if Jesus would only bow down and worship him. Jesus does not deny the Devil's right to these kingdoms. The kingdoms of the world belong to the Devil through man's allegiance to him (2 Cor. 4:4) and he can give them to whom he pleases. Jesus resists Satan's rebellion, saying, "Go, Satan! For it is written, 'You shall worship the Lord your God, and serve Him only (Mt. 4:10, quoting Dt. 6:13, cf. Dt. 10:20).'"[44] Deuteronomy, from which Jesus quotes in his rebuttals against Satan's temptations, is the Suzerain-vassal treaty between God and Israel through which God will establish the kingdom of Israel by the king of His choosing, Jesus. Jesus rests in the words of God's covenant rather than the temptations of Satan. In essence, then, Satan offers Jesus dominion in his humanity over the mediatorial kingdom (creation) which God has prepared for him, but apart from the means that God provided of receiving it—apart from obedience to the revealed will of God—which would disqualify him from being God's perfect, righteous, and faithful human administrator.

After his temptation, Jesus began to preach the gospel of the kingdom to the Jews: "Repent, for the kingdom of heaven is at hand (Mt. 4:17)." This message is consistently preached throughout the first part of Jesus' ministry to the Jews alone.[45] John the Baptist (Mt. 3:1-2), Jesus (Mt. 4:17), the twelve disciples (Mt. 10:5-7), and the 70 disciples (Lk. 10:1, 9) all preached the kingdom to the Jews and not the Gentiles. His message and miracles were geared toward forcing Israel

---

[44] For a fuller handling of the temptation of Christ, see the author's notes on the topic at www.tacomagracebc.org/life-of-messiah-1/05

[45] Importantly, this is not the epistolary Gospel of Salvation, which requires only faith (Act. 16:31; 1 Cor. 15:1-4). The gospel of the kingdom required repentance for Israel while it was offered because they had abandoned the written Law of Moses in exchange for the Oral Law of the Pharisees, and to receive the One who fulfills the Law of Moses, they would have to change their mind about what the Law required. Their national unwillingness to repent of their reinterpretation of the Law became the major stumbling block leading to national unbelief and rejection.

to decide about His person, to reject him or receive him as the Messianic King to rule over Israel on the throne of David.[46, 47]

The Kingdom Rejected

Although early reception of Jesus was positive, the religious and political leaders (Pharisees, Sadducees) had set themselves against Jesus. They made many attempts to discredit Jesus, to expose Him as a fraud, or frame Him as breaking the law of Moses. This came to a climax in the twelfth chapter of Matthew when Jesus cast a demon causing muteness out of a demonized man (Mt. 12:22). The crowd which witnessed Jesus cleanse the demonized man asked, "This man cannot be the Son of David, can he (v. 23)?"[48] The syntax of this question indicates their lack of faith by anticipating a negative answer. The use of *μήτι* (a form of *μή*) instead of *οὐ* in the question, indicates that the speaker expected a negative answer, as A. T. Robertson explains, "If an affirmative or negative answer is expected, then that fact is shown using *οὐ* for the question expecting an affirmative reply and by *μή* for the negative answer. As a matter of fact, any answer may

---

[46] Arnold G. Fruchtenbaum, *Yeshua: The Life of Messiah from a Messianic Jewish Perspective*, Vol. 2, (San Antonio, TX: Ariel Ministries, 2017), 33-34.

[47] This kingdom has not here in any way been redefined or disconnected from the Old Testament which promised a national and physical kingdom to the physical descendants of Abraham, with David's seed ruling from Jerusalem over the promised land and the whole world for eternity future. It would have been deceptive of Jesus to offer to national Israel a spiritual kingdom without qualifying that this kingdom is not the national theocracy which they had rightly anticipated for millennia. To reinterpret Jesus' kingdom offer as anything but the national Messianic kingdom is to do great damage to the text and depart from a literal-historical-grammatical-contextual interpretation. Just as Jesus said, "From the days of John the Baptist until now the kingdom of heaven suffers violence, and violent men take it by force (Mt. 11:12);" so it has been since that time, that many (including much of Christendom) who are not Israel have tried to interpret the kingdom as their own inheritance apart from national Israel.

[48] This reaction by the people demonstrates their expectation that only the promised Messiah would be capable of performing such a miracle. Dr. Arnold Fruchtenbaum lists this among three other miracles which he designates *Messianic Miracles*. Fruchtenbaum, *Yeshua,* vol. 1, 137–149.

be given. It is only the expectation that is presented by *οὐ* or *μή*."[49] Thus, while these Jews saw Jesus demonstrate his Messiahship, they did not believe that the evidence could be trusted for the conclusion that he was the promised seed of David. Though they saw Jesus perform signs associated with the kingdom, they were still in disbelief. The people had listened to the Pharisees and doubted Jesus. They had submitted their wills to the persuasion of the religious leaders who had deceived them. They did not receive the king of God's choosing.

Finally, in Matthew 12:24 the Pharisees make a wicked accusation against Jesus. They accuse Him of casting out demons in the power of the ruler of the demons—Beelzebub—Satan. So terrible is this accusation, that Jesus considers this sin as unpardonable (Mt. 12:31-32) and withdraws the offer of the kingdom from first century Israel, later explaining, "But woe to you, scribes and Pharisees, hypocrites, because you shut off the kingdom of heaven[50] from people; for you do not enter in yourselves, nor do you allow those who are entering to go in (Mt. 23:13)." They had rejected the king, and with Him the offer of the kingdom. The offer of the kingdom of heaven is not again extended to that "evil and adulterous generation (Mt. 12:39)," first century Israel. Rejecting the king of God's choosing based on demon possession was the unpardonable sin for which that generation would come under judgment. That judgment was executed in 70 A.D. in Rome's the Sack of Jerusalem (Lk. 21:20-24).[51]

The offer to the Jews had been sincere: repent and the kingdom will appear. Because of Israel's rejection, the offer was withdrawn, not

---

[49] Robertson cites this verse as an example of this rule. Robertson, A. T., *A Grammar of the Greek New Testament in Light of Historical Research*, (Nashville, TN: Broadman Press, 1934), 917.

[50] The kingdom of heaven refers to its origin and is not an indication of a spiritualized or immaterial kingdom. The term appears only in the book of Matthew, likely out of sensitivity to its Jewish audience and their reticence to write the name of God. It is not distinct from the Kingdom of God on earth through the Messiah, Jesus Christ.

[51] Fruchtenbaum, *Yeshua*, vol. 2, 498.

to return until Israel turns to Jesus in faith to receive Him as their king. "For I say to you, from now on you will not see Me until you say, 'Blessed is He who comes in the name of the Lord (Mt. 23:39)!'" But the failures of man do not disrupt the plans of God. Jesus began immediately to train His disciples for His departure. He was about to "make lemonade out of lemons" by using the believers of first century Israel (the remnant of Israel) to bring in the fulness of the Gentiles (Rom. 11:25) in the time between His departure and return.

The Church

The arrival of the Church and the dispersion of the nation-state of Israel (for a time, in punishment for covenant disobedience under the cursing clause of the Mosaic Covenant) caused many in Christendom to reinterpret the church as superseding Israel and fulfilling the kingdom promises.[52] For this to be possible, plain-sense

---

[52] So Hodge. Charles Hodge, *Systematic Theology*, vol. 2, (Grand Rapids, MI: Eerdmans, 1975), 596–7, 604–5, 8.

So Berkhof. Lewis Berkhof, *Systematic Theology*, 4th revised ed., (Grand Rapids, MI: Eerdmans, 1949), 406.

So Grudem who cites Ladd, but adds, "As the church proclaims the good news of the kingdom, people will come into the church and begin to experience the blessings of God's rule in their lives. The kingdom manifests itself through the church, and thereby the future reign of God breaks into the present. Wayne Grudem, *Systematic Theology: An Introduction to Biblical Doctrine*, (Grand Rapids, MI: Zondervan, 1994), 863–4.

So Gentry, who writes, "Upon His coronation Christ begins ruling judicially over the nations of the earth *through spiritual means* [emphasis original] rather than by the sword. He rules representatively through his people. Those who are redeemed are members of His kingdom. As they labor for Him, they rule by spiritual and ethical power. Their goal? To see all nations baptized in Christ. The essence of Christ's kingdom is spiritual and ethical, not political and racial. Kenneth L. Gentry, Jr., *He Shall Have Dominion: A Postmillennial Eschatology*, 2nd ed., (Tyler, TX: Institute for Christian Economics, 1997), 239.

So Davis, who writes, "…the Kingdom is essentially *a spiritual sphere of divine rescue and restoration* [emphasis original], a sphere in which the evil sons of Satan have been supernaturally transformed into the holy and righteous sons of God. This one Kingdom comes in two stages, separated by a single Consummation at the Parousia of Christ at the end of the present evil age. The first stage is called

scripture must be spiritualized, and a special hermeneutic for prophetic texts must be adopted to allegorize unfulfilled prophecy. This has influenced many in the Church not to believe in the literal fulfillment of scripture, even though all scripture regarding Christ's first advent was fulfilled literally. Thus, an investigation into the domain of the Church, as defined by scripture, becomes necessary.

Lewis Sperry Chafer called the Church an "intercalation" in God's plan, meaning an interruption, or better, a parenthetical event. The Church was not a plan "B," but a temporary pause in God's outworking of the Davidic and Theocratic Kingdom, with the purpose of bringing Gentiles into the promises of the Kingdom by way of the New Covenant in Christ's blood (Eph. 2:11–22). God's plan for Israel is ultimately to rule over creation and must comprise of people from all nations.

Far from being an interruption in God's plan, the Church is only an interruption in His progress with Israel until He has procured a redeemed people from all the nations. Chafer also had this to say of

---

the Kingdom of the Son. During this time, the Messianic Son of God reigns from heaven, by the Spirit, over his earthly subjects. His benevolent rule is spiritual, invisible, redemptive, infinitely valuable, and worthy of all self-sacrifice… sinners enter it spiritually and invisibly by hearing the Gospel message with faith. When at last the Kingdom of the Son has permeated the whole earth—when the Gospel has reached all nations, and a believing people has been gathered out of them—the end will come… The Kingdom of the Father is the second, last, and eternal stage of the Kingdom. Here God's benevolent redemptive rule extends to the physical side of the creation, as well." Dean Davis, *The High King of Heaven: Discovering the Master Keys to the Great End Time Debate*, Enumclaw, WA: Redemption Press, 2014), 139–140.

Many dispensationalists have argued for a mystery facet to the kingdom but deny that the church is a fulfillment of the mediatorial kingdom as anticipated through Israel in the Old Testament. See Charles Ryrie, *Basic Theology*, 398. A comprehensive handling of this view is found by one of its proponents, Arnold Fruchtenbaum. Fruchtenbaum, *Israelology*, 564–6. For a dispensational argument against this view see Woods, *The Coming Kingdom,* 137–140.

the Church in relation to Israel and of Israel and the Church in relation to an earthly kingdom during the present Age of Grace:

> The agelong Jewish advantage because of divine election is, for an age, set aside and the Apostle declares, "There is no difference." They are as individuals alike with the Gentiles "under sin" (Rom. 3:9), and as individuals alike with the Gentiles in that God is rich in mercy to all that call upon Him (Rom. 10:12). This is a new message to Gentiles and equally new to Jews. The divine favor proffered to Gentiles does not consist in offering them a share in the national blessings of Israel, nor does it provide a way whereby the Jew may realize the specific features of his national covenants. Though present salvation is into the kingdom of God (John 3:3), no earthly kingdom is now being offered to any people.[53]

The Church is a new and unique work of God, not a fulfillment of promises from the Old Testament. In the Ephesian letter, Paul reveals that the Church was a mystery. The Church is a mystery, not because it is a spiritual fulfillment of the kingdom, but because it had not been revealed in the Old Testament, making it impossible for it to be the fulfillment of Old Testament prophecy.

The prophet Daniel defines a mystery as that which God alone can reveal—that which cannot be understood by observation. Daniel says to Nebuchadnezzar, "As for the mystery about which the king has inquired, neither wise men, conjurers, magicians nor diviners are able to declare it to the king. However, there is a God in heaven who reveals mysteries, and He has made known to King Nebuchadnezzar what will take place in the latter days (Dan. 2:27–28)." Paul defines it in the same way in the book of Ephesians, saying,

> ...by revelation there was made known to me the mystery, as I wrote before in brief. By referring to this, when you read you can understand my insight into the mystery of

[53] Chafer, Dispensationalism, 30.

> Christ, which in other generations was not made known to the sons of men, as it has now been revealed to His holy apostles and prophets in the Spirit. (Eph. 3:3–6)

In the biblical sense of the word, a mystery is unknowable until the time it is divinely revealed, being unobservable in general revelation, and requiring special revelation to make it known. This naturally makes *mysteries* the first time something is divinely revealed. The kingdom, on the other hand, was not a mystery. Much of the prophetic writing of the Old Testament is dedicated to revelation concerning the kingdom. A mystery revealed in the New Testament cannot be the fulfillment of an Old Testament promise. The fact that Paul defines the Church as a mystery, not revealed until the New Testament, disqualifies it from functioning as the fulfillment of Old Testament prophecy.

The purpose of the Church is different than that of the kingdom. The Church is not the kingdom; it has no mandate to rule over creation or humanity. It has three duties: to evangelize the lost world (Mt. 28:18–20) with the Gospel of God's grace toward sinful man provided because of His love by the blood of Jesus; to edify the body of Christ (Eph. 4:11–16) through teaching, learning, reproving, and growing in love and fellowship while we await the return of Jesus; and to exult God (Eph. 3:21) by ascribing Him the glory and worship which He rightly deserves.

Larkin has this to say of the mystery of the Church and its purpose:

> The "mystery" was, that God was going to form an entirely "new thing" composed of both "Jew" and "Gentile," to be called the "Church." The purpose of this dispensation is seen in the "divine program" outlined by the Apostle James in his address to the first Church council held at Jerusalem (Acts 15:13–18), where he declares that God has visited the Gentiles to "take out of them 'a people' for His name." The purpose of this dispensation then is not the bringing in

> of the kingdom, or the conversion of the world, but the gathering out of an "elect body," the Church.[54]

Larkin continues, drawing this major distinction between national Israel and the body of Christ: "While Israel is a 'called out body' it is a 'National Body,' composed exclusively of the descendants of Abraham, but the Church is not a 'National Body,' for it is not composed of the people of any one nation, but of individuals from every kindred, people, tribe and nation."[55] The Church is neither the kingdom, nor does it replace Israel in its kingdom promises. Only the nation of Israel can fulfill the kingdom promises, and the Church is not Israel.[56]

The Kingdom's Inauguration

The kingdom is dependent upon Israel receiving the king of God's choosing. After Jesus was rejected by first century Israel, the

---

[54] Larkin, *Rightly Dividing the Word,* 45–46. Bold and all-caps removed from original for readability.

[55] Ibid, 46.

[56]Dr. Steve Cook summarizes the differences between the church and Israel. A simple comparison between the characteristics of the church and Israel will show the utter divide in the plan of both these spiritual bodies. Israel is a nation (Ex. 19:6); the church is not (Rom. 10:19). God's program for Israel focused on the land (Gen. 12:1; 15:18; 17:8); the church is called to go out to many lands (Matt. 28:19–20; Acts 1:8). Israel was recognized by other nations (Num. 14:15; Josh 5:1); the church was a mystery not known in the Old Testament (Eph. 3:1–6; Col. 1:26–27; cf. Rom 16:25–26). Israel was under the Law of Moses (John 1:17); the church is under the law of Christ (1 Cor. 9:21; Gal. 6:2). Israel had a priesthood that was specific to the tribe of Levi (Num. 3:6–7); all Christians are priests to God (Rev. 1:6). Israel worshipped first at the Tabernacle and later the Temple (Ex. 40:18–38; 2 Ch. 8:14–16); the body of the Christian is the temple of the Lord and believers gather locally where they want (1 Cor. 6:19-20; cf. Col. 4:15). Israel offered animal sacrifices to God (Lev. 4:1–35); Christians offer spiritual sacrifices (1 Pet. 2:5; cf. Rom. 12:1; Heb 13:15). Israel was required to tithe from the produce of their land (Deut. 14:22–23, 28-29; Num. 18:21); no tithe is required from Christians, only a joyful attitude when giving (2 Cor. 9:7). Dr. Steven R. Cook, www.thinkingscripture.com.

kingdom was put in a state of postponement. While the kingdom awaits the conversion of Israel, a new and distinct entity—the Church—occupies God's focus. The Church will be removed from the earth at a time in the future and God's attention will return to Israel.

Prophecy looks forward to the final Gentile kingdom of Daniel 2 and 7: the feet of iron and clay and the terrible beast. That final government will be ruled by the False Messiah, who will come into power promising peace and security to unbelieving Israel (Dan. 9:27). Coincidentally, Israel, who rejected Jesus, will accept this man (Jn. 5:43). This is the man whom Satan will finally propose as His own Mediatorial King over the earth—the man of perdition—whom Satan will indwell and in the futility of his own hubris he will seek to solidify his hold over physical earth and usurp God as its ruler through conforming creation to his own will rather than to God's.

That future time will be one of unspeakable persecution upon Israel as Satan seeks to crush those who are alone responsible to enthrone God's king physically on earth. Through that persecution by Satan's False Messiah, Israel will finally be converted (Rom. 11:25–27), confessing their national sin of rejecting the king of God's choosing (Lev. 26:40–42; Hos. 5:15); receive Jesus as their king and call on him for physical salvation from the predations of Satan's counterfeit king (Zech. 12:10; Mt. 23:37–39).[57]

Just as God cannot fulfill his promises to this world by creating another universe, so He cannot fulfill His promises to Israel through any other nation. He has drawn Israel into His purpose of a Mediatorial Kingdom on earth, and Jesus must reign as king over Israel if he shall ever reign over this earth. Any other throne but the throne of David would invalidate God's word and make Him a liar. Israel will be converted and receive her king. Jesus will return to rescue Israel, conquer the armies of the False Messiah, destroying his counterfeit kingdom and his reign over this earth. As the conquered foe, he will be

---

[57]Fruchtenbaum, *Israelology*, 717–24.

incarcerated, and Jesus will rule over all of creation from the kingdom of Israel on the throne of David for one thousand years.

The book of Revelation reveals the impossibility of Satan's venture, for when the Throne Room of God is revealed (from which God rules eternally), the reader is presented with a book which the One sitting on the throne holds in His hand. It is the title deed to the earth[58] and His creation—the domain over which God's Mediatorial King presides. And Jesus alone has proven worthy to take the scroll from the hand of God the Father. Jesus, the second Adam, who was tested in all the ways which man is, and yet without sin—Jesus the Lion of Judah and the Root of David—Jesus the Son with whom God is well pleased, opens the scroll and assumes authority over his birthright: the mediatorial throne of God's created universe.

This is the end of the middle civilization of God's plan. Satan's Babel has reemerged from the shadows and little by little, Jesus strips Satan of his foothold on the earth while amassing to himself countless millions even in the final hours of *the world that now is* (Rev. 7). The world that is to come will see Jesus fulfill God's purpose for creation by implementing God's will perfectly over all creation, destroying all that rebels against God's will.

During the thousand years which Satan will be in chains, Jesus will fulfill all of God's purposes in creation. He will take up the mantle of the Theocratic Administrator and God will have been victorious on earth. This earthly kingdom will be made up of all those who have been saved by the blood of Jesus in all ages, including the redeemed who survived the Tribulation in mortal bodies, and those who died and were resurrected. Those who are resurrected are resurrected into glorified bodies. However, those who survived the Tribulation will not have glorified bodies, and neither will their children. They will repopulate the earth, finally fulfilling God's purpose for creation that man be fruitful and fill the earth (Gen. 1:28, cf. the numerousness of the rebel party in Rev. 20:8) while a man sits on the throne of earth.

---

[58] Alva J. McClain, *The Greatness of the Kingdom,* (Winona Lk, IN: BMH Books, 1959), 472–3.

Many of those children, even under the direct rule of Jesus, will rebel against God. At the end of the 1,000-year reign of Jesus, Satan will be unchained to lead a rebellion against Jesus the king, coopting the millennial nation of Magog as his new governmental puppet after Babylon's total destruction and absence from the Millennial kingdom. At that time, Satan's ambitions will be finally and fully destroyed, and he will be cast into the lake of fire for eternity, along with those who rebelled with him (Rev. 20:7–10).

After the rebellion and Jesus' final victory, Jesus will hand mediation of creation over to God the Father. The mediatorial and universal thrones will merge (Rev. 22:1), and God will create a new heaven and a new earth which will be an eternal dwelling for man with God.

Conclusion

God must be victorious on this earth before it can pass away. History traces the fulfillment of His original plan for creation in the King, Jesus Christ. When history is viewed within the confines of eternity, it becomes apparent that God's glory is always at the forefront, and in all ways, Jesus is the exact representation of His glory (Heb. 1:3). Creation can only be fulfilled through His mediatorship; His promises to Israel can only be fulfilled through His Messiahship; and salvation can only be achieved through His mortal flesh and divine nature, His blood poured out to pay for the sins of the whole world. He alone is worthy of the throne over God's creation, because He alone has shown Himself perfect and obedient to God's will in every way.

> Worthy are You to take the book and to break its seals; for You were slain, and purchased for God with Your blood men from every tribe and tongue and people and nation. You have made them to be a kingdom and priests to our God; and they will reign upon the earth. (Rev. 5:9b–10)

Bibliography

Berkhof, Lewis. *Systematic Theology.* 4th Revised Edition. Grand Rapids, MI: Eerdmans, 1949.

Chafer, Lewis Sperry. *Dispensationalism.* Dallas, Texas: Dallas Seminary Press, 1951.

———. *Systematic Theology.* 8 Volumes. Dallas, TX: Dallas Seminary Press, 1947.

Constable, Tom. *Tom Constable's Expository Notes on the Bible.* Galaxie Software, 2003.

Davis, Dean. *The High King of Heaven: Discovering the Master Keys to the Great End Time Debate.* Enumclaw, WA: Redemption Press, 2014.

France, R. T. *Matthew: An Introduction and Commentary, Vol. 1, Tyndale New Testament Commentaries.* Downers Grove, IL: InterVarsity Press, 1985.

Fruchtenbaum, Arnold G. *Israelology: The Missing Link in Systematic Theology.* Revised 2020 Edition. San Antonio, TX: Ariel Ministries, 1989.

———. *Yeshua: The Life of Messiah from a Messianic Jewish Perspective.* 4 Volumes. San Antonio, TX: Ariel Ministries, 2017.

Gentry, Kenneth L. Jr. *He Shall Have Dominion: A Postmillennial Eschatology.* 2nd Edition. Tyler, TX: Institute for Christian Economics, 1997.

Gentry, Peter J., and Stephen J. Wellum. *God's Kingdom through God's Covenants: A Concise Biblical Theology.* Wheaton, IL: Crossway, 2015.

Grudem, Wayne. *Systematic Theology: An Introduction to Biblical Doctrine.* Grand Rapids, MI: Zondervan, 1994.

Hodge, Charles. *Systematic Theology.* 3 Volumes. Grand Rapids, MI: Eerdmans, 1975.

Johnson, Elliot. *A Dispensational Biblical Theology*. Allen, TX: Bold Grace Ministries, 2016.

Larkin, Clarence. *Dispensational Truth, or "God's Plan and Purpose in the Ages": Charts*. Philadelphia, PA: Clarence Larkin, 1918.

———. *Rightly Dividing the Word*. Philadelphia, PA: Clarence Larkin, 1921.

McClain, Alva J. *The Greatness of the Kingdom*. Winona Lake, IN: BMH Books, 1959.

Merrill, Eugene H., Rooker, Mark F., and Grisanti, Michael A. *The Word and the World: An Introduction to the Old Testament*. Nashville, TN: B&H Publishing Group, 2011.

Morgan, G. Campbell. *The Analyzed Bible: The Book of Genesis*, vol. 9. New York; Chicago; Toronto; London; Edinburgh: Fleming H. Revell Company, 1911.

Pentecost, J. Dwight. *Thy Kingdom Come: Tracing God's Kingdom Program and Covenant Promises Throughout History*. Wheaton, IL: Victor Books, 1990.

Peters, George N. H. *The Theocratic Kingdom*. 3 Volumes. Grand Rapids, MI: Kregel Publications, 1972.

Robertson, A. T. *A Grammar of the Greek New Testament in the Light of Historical Research*. Nashville, TN. Broadman Press, 1934.

Ross, Allen P. "Genesis," in *The Bible Knowledge Commentary: An Exposition of the Scriptures*, Edited by J. F. Walvoord and R. B. Zuck, Vol. 1. Wheaton, IL: Victor Books, 1985.

Ryrie, Charles Caldwell. *Basic Theology: A Popular Systematic Guide to Understanding Biblical Truth*. Chicago, IL: Moody Press, 1999.

Thieme, Jr. R. B. *Thieme's Bible Doctrine Dictionary*, Houston, TX: R. B. Thieme Jr. Bible Ministries, 2022.

Woods, Andrew. *The Coming Kingdom: What Is the Kingdom and How is Kingdom Now Theology Changing the Focus of the Church?* Duluth, MN: Grace Gospel Press, 2016.

Joseph's Tasks in Egypt

By Donald Thomas

When most people read the story of Joseph in Genesis, the normal thought is he was sent to Egypt to save the family of God from the coming famine. I think there are several other reasons why God sent Joseph to Egypt. A careful reading of the account in Genesis 37–50 will reveal those other reasons. Let's explore the Scripture together to discover those reasons.

The Youthful Joseph (Chapter 37)

Even though Joseph was born long after the "first born", he enjoyed the status of the "favorite son". He knew it, his father knew it and most of all his brothers knew it and were infuriated by it. Jacob even made Joseph a special coat to tell the world of Joseph's special status.

Seventeen-year-old Joseph, either on purpose or innocently, heaped wood on that burning hatred. He tattled on his older brothers to his father. He had a prophetic dream of ruling over his brothers and told them about the dream. I can imagine that he told them in an arrogant teen-age way. This caused the brother to hate him even more.

Later he had another dream of ruling over his father, mother, and brothers and told them about it as well. He should have learned from the response of the brothers to his first dream. With jealousy added to the hatred, the brothers left to herd the flocks rather than put up with the arrogance of Joseph.

The time at Shechem must have been like a vacation away from Joseph, his coat, and his dreams. But, as all good things must end, here comes Joseph, coat and all, over the hill looking for them. As Joseph was coming toward them they were planning on how to get rid of him. The plan was simple. Kill him, throw the body into one of the cisterns, and put the covering back over it. Reuben, the oldest son, was not all for the plan. He suggested rather than kill him, just throw him in the cistern and let nature take care of the rest. Ruben was planning to come back later and get Joseph out of the pit. Reuben wasn't that tender-hearted. His motive was to get back into his father's good graces as the "first born" after he had fallen out by sleeping with Bilhah, Jacob's concubine.

Joseph arrived. The brothers stripped him of his coat and threw him in the cistern. Then they were preparing to sit down to eat. With their brother pleading with them from the cistern they still had an appetite. The plan then changed to selling Joseph to some of Uncle Ismael's traders who just "happened by" at that time.

What can be gleaned from the activities reported in Genesis 37?

- The father did not establish and promote harmony in the family. He openly showed his favoritism for Joseph with the coat and job assignments. Joseph, the baby brother, was the apple of his father's eye. Everyone knew it. The brothers despised Joseph for it. This was a far cry from proper leadership of a family.
- Joseph did not display humility. He didn't seem to know when to keep his mouth shut. He added to the reasons his brothers hated him by reporting their bad behavior back to the father (tattling) and telling of his dreams (bragging).
- The brothers showed a coarse and uncaring nature toward their brother and disrespect for the family reputation. They were evidently doing bad things that Joseph felt needed to be reported to their father. They threw him into the cistern then sat down to lunch while listening to his screams from the cistern. They invented a lie to tell Jacob about what happened to his favorite son. I'm sure the money paid by the Ishmaelites did not wind up in the family bank account. These were not actions appropriate for the future leaders of the twelve tribes of Israel.

The Slave Joseph (Chapters 39–40)

After his arrival in Egypt, Joseph was bought by Potiphar, a high ranking official in Pharaoh's court. He quickly rose to a position of great responsibility being put in charge of Potiphar's entire household. When approached by Potiphar's wife for sexual favors, he resisted her advances. She grew impatient with his refusal to accommodate her and falsely accused him of attempted rape. This resulted in him being thrown into prison.

While in prison, Joseph remained a faithful servant and again quickly rose to a position of authority. He was in charge of the entire prison. During this time, he properly interpreted the dreams of two of his fellow prisoners, the chief butler and the chief baker. When both interpretations came true, Joseph asked the chief butler to mention him to Pharaoh. The butler promptly forgot about Joseph.

What can be gleaned from the activities reported in Genesis 39-40?

- Even though Joseph was loyal to his masters and quickly rose to positions of authority, he still needed time to learn some humility. God left him in prison to learn this lesson.
- Even though God gave Joseph the ability to interpret dreams, God caused the butler to "forget" about Joseph to give him more time to fully learn these lessons.
- Joseph maintained his faith and loyalty toward God. He accepted his lot in life even though he did not understand why these things were happening to him. Especially since he undoubtedly remembered the dreams, he was convinced that came from God.

The Redeemed Joseph (Chapter 41)

As time passed, Pharaoh had two dreams that disturbed him greatly. No one in the court could interpret his dreams. The butler suddenly remembers about Joseph's ability to interpret dreams and informs Pharaoh the Hebrew slave that has this ability.

Pharaoh calls for Joseph to be brought in. Joseph interprets the dreams and humbly provides Pharaoh with a plan of action to avoid the coming famine in Egypt. He gave the glory for his ability to God and did not even hint at him having a part in the plan. Pharaoh agrees to the plan and immediately appoints Joseph to administer of that plan. Joseph becomes the number two ruler of all Egypt.

Joseph surveys the land and prepares the details needed to implement the plan. He is so successful that people from all the lands start coming to Egypt for food. Joseph had stockpiled enough grain during the seven years of plenty to supply Egypt as well as all the surrounding countries with grain during the seven years of famine.

What can be gleaned from the activities reported in Genesis 41?

- During his two additional years of waiting, Joseph finally learned humility. He humbly interpreted the dreams of Pharaoh and gave the credit for this ability to God. He also provided a plan. He did not even consider including himself in the administration of the plan.
- God caused the butler to "remember" Joseph. After two years of "forgetting", the butler suddenly "remembers" about Joseph and tells Pharaoh.
- God caused the Pharaoh to place Joseph in charge of the plan. Pharaoh recognized Joseph's God given ability and puts him in position as the number two ruler in all Egypt. Joseph, now humble and obedient, is successful in his efforts in this pagan land. The plan is accomplished, and Egypt has enough grain to survive the famine and to sell grain to other people in surrounding countries.

The Teaching Joseph (Chapter 42)

As the famine intensified, the brothers finally come to Egypt to buy grain. Since Joseph now dresses and talks like an Egyptian, the brothers do not recognize him. After all, it has been 22 years since they sold Joseph into slavery.

With his identity hidden, Joseph puts the brothers through several tests to see if they had any remorse about what they did to him. He accuses them of being spies. He demands they bring Benjamin to him. He holds Simeon in prison between the two trips to Egypt. The guilt of the brothers causes them to conclude that God is punishing them for what they did to Joseph.

On the second trip, he brings them to his house for dinner. He puts his cup in Benjamin's sack and has Benjamin arrested. Judah requests that he be placed in prison and Benjamin be released to return to his father.

Joseph sees that the brothers were truly sorry about their past actions toward him and had changed their heart attitude. He reveals his true identity to them and invites the whole family to join him in Egypt. The family of Israel is saved from the ravages of the famine. They are given a place of seclusion in the land of Goshen where they become a numerous nation free from the pagan influences of the surrounding Egyptians.

What can be gleaned from the activities reported in Genesis 42?

- Joseph not only saves Israel from the famine, he is instrumental in the heart change of the brothers to make them appropriate leaders of the twelve tribes of Israel. They are no longer the coarse and uncaring men that sold their brother into slavery.
- The brothers demonstrate their care and concern for their father and Benjamin. They were willing to take the punishment that Joseph proposed for Benjamin. They did not want to cause any further sorrow for their father.

- God works all things for the good of those that love and serve Him even though those things seem bad at the time. He used Joseph's tests of the brothers to instill a kinder heart attitude in the brothers.
- God's plans for people are not thwarted by the actions of those people. He is able to make their actions, as bad as they may be, work for His ultimate good and glory.

Generous Living

Generosity Within the Church

By Randy Peterman

As the New Testament saint is not under the Law with its greater than 10% taxes on observant Jews (specifically the so-called 10% tithe), the believer needs to understand what is revealed for practical application around stewardship, the needs of the body, and financial obligations for the church. This does not mean that we ignore the Old Testament's principles, but that we need to understand what clear doctrines need appropriation for the New Testament saint who is looking to be obedient to the Holy Spirit, biblical revelation, and looking to love their co-heirs in Christ through stewardship of God's ministry through them.

Giving Throughout the Old Testament

It is worth at least a cursory glance at the doctrines around generosity throughout the Bible to see God's direction, God's faithfulness, and the impact of generosity throughout God's direction for saints. We need to understand what worldly possession looks like in light of God's role as sovereign creator. We need to understand what currency represents. We need to understand the purpose of the Tithe as outlined in the Old Testament as well as how many tithes there were (the answer may surprise you). If we're going to quote the Old Testament doctrines we should understand them in context. We should also understand what the New Testament teaches about stewardship in contrast to the Old Testament.

God as Creator/Owner

Fundamentally all Biblical doctrine around ownership, stewardship, and possession are rooted in the idea that God, as creator, was owner. Not a molecule on the planet was outside of His creation and outside of His ownership. His giving of stewardship and dominion of the earth and its domain to Adam (Gen. 1:28) was forfeited at the fall (Gen. 3:17–24, the world would resist mankind, and food would become toilsome). When God repeats the concept of multiplying (filling/swarming) over the earth to Noah, dominion and subduing are not part of the command. Animals would become afraid of mankind (Gen. 9:7), further separating mankind's previous dominion from present reality. The ease of Adam in the garden was shockingly different from the efforts required today to provide food for each human being, despite technology.

God was owner, and so all things were subject to Him, and any dominion or stewardship given was done so within His purview and within the limitation of God's gifting of that creation to mankind. All offerings and gifts back to Him, or to others within creation, were given because of His mercy.[59] This means that for any person walking the earth from day 6 onward, we have been entirely dependent on God for every breath, all our needs, and we have not, of our own strength, power or accord, been able to declare our own wealth.

Side Trip: What is currency?

As we move forward through this study we're going to be talking about stewardship. This is assuming that our time and resources have value, and that currency represents that value. In economics books currency sometimes is falsely described as a trading medium where one person has potatoes, another person has shoes, but it's possible that the person with potatoes does not need shoes so currency gives them an agreed upon tool for exchange. Anthropologists find no evidence of this trading mechanism. *Instead we find that currency was developed to represent the value of life and life energy.*[60] This principle carries throughout cultures, and history, and can be seen through ideas like dowries [where wealth was traded in exchange for lives and descendants],

---

[59] Defined as: God's disposition to kindness, rooted in love (Psa. 86:15; 145:8; Lk. 6:36; Eph. 2:4; Heb. 2:17; Jas. 5:11)

[60] When we consider that currency represents life energy it removes plebian explanations of pies and a limited understanding of global wealth and wealth generation.

sacrifices, and even in Jacob and Esau where Jacob sent livestock ahead to Esau amounting to hundreds of thousands of dollars at today's market value.[61]

What is Stewardship?

A steward is someone who has agency or managerial responsibility of someone else's property or resources. Stewardship is the doctrinal idea that since God is owner/creator of everything in all of creation we may have some responsibility for a sub-set of that, but it's ultimately His. This concept challenges us to say things like my (Randy) friend Tony once said on a phone call, "Someone rear-ended God's car." If we understand that everything we own is God's, then the concept of stewardship demands of us that we reflect on what He would want us to do with it. As New Testament saints indwelt by the Holy Spirit, renewing our minds about what we have a stewardship over, we can relax our fists and with open hands pray for His direction in stewardship.

God's Supernatural Work Through Stewardship

An important principle around life as a whole is that God is doing something supernatural through His creation and those with His likeness specifically. This is why He can bless and bless and bless and never run out of blessings within this world. This is why we should look at stewardship with excited anticipation: What awe-inspiring thing is God going to do next in His saints?

Cain killed Able (Gen. 4:3–16) because he had not observed God's supernatural provision and offered a lesser offering and was jealous. Instead of observing an opportunity for awe, he was selfish and that selfishness led to jealousy, murder, judgment, and a curse. In

---

[61] See one calculation of $654,960 from https://thenotesaregood.com/tag/jacobs-gift-to-esau-costly/. Some have estimated that the value would be higher because at the time animal husbandry and agricultural difficulties were greater due to the technological disparity.

contrast to this we find Abraham (Gen. 13; 14:17-24) and David (1 Chron. 21:24; 2 Sam. 9) living with incredible generosity because they were in awe of God's amazingness. Within the founding of the New Testament church the generosity between saints made it so that Dr. Luke wrote that they shared their possessions in such a way that they had everything in common and gave as there were needs (Acts 2:44–45; 4:32–35). This liberality among the saints is a principle of understanding and mindset: I am a vessel with a stewardship over things that God is using.

When Ananias and Saphira (Acts 5:1–11) lied to Peter and the Holy Spirit and were struck dead it scared the church because they saw God's wrath on those who try to lie to Him. We don't propose that everyone sell everything they have (acts is descriptive, not prescriptive after all), but we strongly suggest that the believer consider the integrity they have with their stewardship and for all that is holy (which is every saint): don't lie about it!

Should We Be Tithing?

While the believer is not under the Law many teachers pull the tithe [usually redefined as 10% given to the church] forward into the New Testament as a guideline or principle. This ignores Paul's admonition to the Galatians (Gal. 5:3) that if you're going to try to do one 613 of the Old Testament Law you must do all 613 Laws. Reaching around the Cross of Jesus to cherry pick parts of the Law rather than clearly teaching New Testament doctrine around giving leaves the believer at a disadvantage as well as the whole body starving for biblical ministry through stewardship empowered by the Holy Spirit in response to grace.

In short, believers should not be strictly adhering to the Law's directions around tithing. We'll dig into what the New Testament saint should be considering instead.

The Tithe was Not 10%

The tithe was not just a generous gift from the Jew to the Levitical priesthood. It was a tax prescribed for the Levites who had no land as an inheritance. It was part of a more complex tax that the obedient Jew was to pay in compliance with the Mosaic covenant with Israel (Dt. 28–29).

- The Levitical tithe was 10% for the Levites for spiritual service and governance throughout the nation (Lev. 27:30–32; Num. 18:21, 24)
- The festival tithe was 10% for the celebration of God's provision (Dt. 14:22-27)
- The three-year charity for the Levite and the poor (Dt. 14:28-29)

The Old Testament tithes combined for an approximately 23% "tax" under the Mosaic Law [10 + 10 + (10/3)]. On top of this the Law demanded lending to those in need with zero interest along with the forgiveness of that loan every seven years (Lev. 25:23-28), offerings and feasts, and other economically impactful practices around food clothing, shelter, hygiene, and work.

It is worth noting that the blessing of God was to be on the observant nation of Israel making the offerings and the tithe a celebration of God's goodness. The tithe was great, but the tithe was for the Old Testament Jew.

The Law was given for Israel in the Land

Assuming that an observant Jew was trying to comply with the commands of the Law, once the nation was taken captive, there were not necessarily places for the people to be observant, Levites to minister, and ways to properly obey the commands. The fact that the Law could not be obeyed was to be a sign of judgment to the nation of Israel that they should repent. The 23% would only be possible while the Lord Blessed the nation in the Land as slavery does not lend itself to obedience to the Law.

While some have cited Abraham's giving 10% to Melchizedek as a tithe before the Law, we don't observe with Job (estimated to be alive around the same time as Abraham) that his uprightness is presented in a tithe, but in offerings to God for sin as well as living generously with his family. Abraham's generosity was an agreement between him and the Lord and it was in response to God's fulfillment of His promise for blessings for Abraham and His descendants. Furthermore, it was by no means regular, nor was it on his life's income, but only based upon the spoils of a single war. Attempting to draw a link between Abraham and the tithe shows just how weak the argument for a Christian tithing really is.

In addition to the tithe being for Israel in the land, the tithe was 10% of everything that God provided, not just currency. If you had any produce that you grew in your garden? Under the Law you need to give 10% of that to your priests.

The Tithe was Given for a Theocracy & Kingdom

God had established the nation of Israel as a theocracy under His heavenly direction to take the nation unto Himself. His earthly representatives were the priesthood that needed God's provision through the blessing to the nation. Once the nation was divided, taken captive, or subdued adherence to the system became even more burdensome, and made for an emphasis on the bondage from disobedience.

The Tithe Had a Tithe

Numbers 18:26 tells that the Levites, who were to collect the tithe as part of their duties, were to offer up one tenth of the tithe. If the tithe is for today pastors ought to collect $1/10^{th}$ of the things put into the offering plates and burn it up on an altar to show the body that they are compliant with the rules around the tithe.

The Law Has No Place of Authority in the Life of the New Testament Believer

As the Apostles Paul stated over and over to the New Testament saints: we are not under the Law (Acts 10:15; 13:39; 18:13; 21:20-21; Rom. 3:28; 7:1-4; 8:2-4; Gal. 3:2, 24–25], and if we try to comply with one part of the Law we must comply with all of the Law (Gal. 5:3). As God moved the church away from the theocracy and into a world-wide body the needs of His people changed radically. Compliance with the Mosaic Law would no longer be possible, and on top of that many things around our economy and geography no longer fit in a cut-and-dried application.

In the Old Testament the Levites were the priests serving God to His set aside people; In the New Testament all saints are priests (Rev. 1:6). You either should have no inheritance like the Levites or you should be giving yourself 10% off the top. Rather, you're not under the Law ministering under the old Deuteronomic covenant but are in a new relationship with Christ as His bride, a kingdom, priests to His God and Father. This leads us to need to understand giving in the New Testament so that we can understand what we do instead of tithing 23 or more percent.

Giving in the New Testament

The New Testament Saint is Called to Abide

As we read through the New Testament, we find that a different motivation is to be underpinning our actions. We no longer see the Law as a driver (it was a school master Galatians 3:24-25 we have died to Romans 7:6). Instead, the principle of Holy Spirit-led living (called Abiding, Beholding or Walking by the Spirit) is our motive. Grace is the thing that drives us to manifest God's work in our lives, not just a mere covering for shortcomings.

The Holy Spirit May Ask Far More Than 10%

One of the problems that many readers run into when reading the New Testament is that there is no restatement of the tithe for the church, nor is there some progressive revelation of an alternative number. This creates difficulty because we want there to be a simple mechanism by which we know we've complied with God's commands. Instead, though, the New Testament saint is to abide and know that God may ask of us far beyond what the Law may ask in loving our neighbor. The flesh wants rules, compliance, and to keep God off our back, but abiding leads to generosity, sharing, and a recognition of stewardship rather than possession. When we look at New Testament doctrine around giving to the Body we find it chock full of people giving outside of percentages and instead giving as need is understood.

Generosity in Light of Need

In our culture today we have a real need for vulnerability around need. Need is treated like a weakness, but the Biblical teachings around need demand a biblical response that reflects a level of intimacy and communion within the body that is not only described but prescribed. Multiple parties are involved with need in the scriptures:

- God, the ultimate owner and provider
- The one in need
- The one with the supply
- Often an agent who can bring the one in need and the supplier together (see the Doctrine of Agency below)

When we look in this context one member of the body is caring for another member of the body with the love of God, the provision of God, and need is not associated with shame, punishment, or condescension.

Since all parties involved see God as using us in His supernatural plan on this earth as His creation and His body generosity and need come hand-in-hand to create a glorifying outworking of the Holy Spirit. The life of Christ is manifested, and the provision of God may very likely bring opportunities to praise God publicly, share the gospel, and celebrate together as a church for God's use of these earthen vessels (2 Cor. 4:5–7).

The Doctrine of Agency

There's an amazing thing that many believers have experienced that comes from need. Paul writes in Philippians 4:18–19:

> [18] But I have received everything in full and have an abundance; I am amply supplied, having received from Epaphroditus what you have sent, a fragrant aroma, an acceptable sacrifice, well-pleasing to God. [19] And my God will supply all your needs according to His riches in glory in Christ Jesus.

There's a lot packed into these few sentences, but one principle we should see is that God may allow us to be agents (or co-stewards) in times of need. If I know that someone has something you need and can help them get it to you, then I am an agent, used of God, like Epaphroditus.

- Epaphroditus had knowledge of the need
- Epaphroditus communicated (in a godly way) that need to the body
- The body responded by the Holy Spirit with a gift
- Epaphroditus carefully carried that gift to Paul

As these things happened who was glorified? God was glorified! God supplied Paul's need, so Paul was praising, but so were the saints in Philippi, so was Epaphroditus, and so have so many other saints since they understood these principles.

Needs need to be known and the body should not expect a 'mind reading pastor.' Open, vulnerable communication is fundamental to body life. The Holy Spirit may move in some to give anonymous, unexpected gifts, but honest, tactical communication with one another about needs may lead to transformative expressions of agape love.

Giving Cheerfully

Paul writes to the wrestling saints in Corinth in 2 Corinthians 9:1–5 that he is excited for their generous giving to the funds for the persecuted and impoverished church in Jerusalem, and that the Macedonians (the region Paul was evangelizing and likely writing the letter from) were encouraged to give. Often teachers move to the next few verses presented in this letter and jump to giving for the church without properly addressing the interpretive issues that this brings with it.

Paul encourages the Corinthians to cheerfully give *extra* towards this fund for the Jerusalem saints. This passage is not about giving cheerfully to the needs of the local body in Corinth, it is about the needs of the saints in Jerusalem. The principles Paul puts forth are not without value to our study but should be understood in light of their proper context.

Bountiful Sewing (2 Cor. 9:6)

Many charlatans have delivered a hearty helping of guilt along with this one verse to "stir hearers to generosity." Some have called it seed faith. If you want to sew $100 God will reward you with $1,000, or $10,000. What they fail to teach is that this is not a principle of promised worldly blessing with some ratio, but is instead probably more closely tied to promises and proverbs like:

> Proverbs 22:9 – The generous will themselves be blessed, for they share their food with the poor.
>
> You shall generously give to him, and your heart shall not be grieved when you give to him, because for this thing the LORD your God will bless you in all your work and in all your undertakings. For the poor will never cease to be in the land; therefore I command you, saying, 'You shall freely

open your hand to your brother, to your needy and poor in your land. (Dt. 15:10–11)

Put another way: you have a stewardship that will impact others in the body. Giving generously to those in need shows that as a steward you are prepared to be obedient in the care of the body. God *may* use that in a way that blesses you in an earthly way to provide more care.

Purposed Giving (v 7a)

Paul calls the saints to give what they had committed [purposed] to giving. Remember that in verse 5 he called them out for having a begrudging attitude in their giving [possibly related to Paul's not having come back through Corinth]. The word translated 'purposed' in the Greek literally means, "To bring out from the stores." Don't bring out from the stores that you didn't intend to bring. No one should coerce you into giving [not out of compulsion].

Cheerful Giving (v 7b)

Finally, the part that gets quoted so often, "God loves a cheerful giver." In light of the power of God in you and your stewardship no amount given by the direction of the Holy Spirit should be anything less than cheerful. Sometimes, though, God will push us to give more than we thought we were going to give. This isn't because it's without cheerfulness, but because the Holy Spirit is moving in us, and our flesh might have had other plans. In more than one conversation and testimony with believers people have recounted stories of God making it clear that they were to give money earmarked for other things and by faith they gave that amount.

Cheerfulness here is willingness and obedience. If you must pay the mortgage tomorrow, but some preacher is trying to get you to plant some seeds, this is not cheerful, it's bad stewardship. However, if you're being compelled by the Holy Spirit to give, His provision will see you through. What should not be happening is that you give to one person in need and become the next person in need by the same amount. Transference of financial problems isn't Paul's goal here.

What if I'm called to cheerfully give 10%?

It's possible that in light of cheerful giving and conviction from the Holy Spirit you will want to give 10%. That's great! It's just not a tithe. For the edification of the saints in your life, don't brag about it, and don't call it a tithe. It may be 10%, but it isn't from the Law, and it may cause them confusion. Instead, urge your co-heirs to be abiding, prayerful, and good stewards of God's resources.

The Spiritual Gift of Giving

When Paul is writing to the church in Rome in Romans 12 he lists off some spiritual giftings (vv. 4–8). All of those gifts come with a stewardship. One of the most important issues in ministry and stewardship is that the Lord first wants us to give of ourselves, and our financial giving is a natural response to that. If we limit our understanding of service to the Lord simply to financially supporting those who go then we really haven't been generous at all in our most valuable resources - our time and our energy. A believer's giving and gifting are all part of the stewardship we have over our entire lives. It is possible for us to squelch the Holy Spirit's movement in our lives. The good news is that if we're walking by the Holy Spirit (v. 1) and we're thinking God's thoughts after Him (vv. 2–3) and if we have the gift of giving – which is not everyone – we should be choosing to give generously!

If this is your spiritual gift, we praise the Lord with you! You have a stewardship that the body needs. Like all spiritual gifts you need to understand it, you need to exercise it, and you need to be abiding so that your giving is from His direction and not the flesh.

Giving in Light of the Operation of the Church

First Corinthians 9:9 tells us that we should not muzzle the ox and then Paul uses that to describe the body giving so that those who are feeding them spiritually may be provided for.[62] Many modern

[62] Which he then states he declined, but the principle still stands.

churches operate well outside of the simple realm of the early church that met in the Synagogues and house-to-house churches. Their overhead was much smaller and their structure was possibly quite different. It is outside the scope of this writing to fully address ecclesiology and various arguments for or against the different church structures that exist, but the principle that we do see Paul writing about here is one that is important: if the saints come together to provide for some of the needs of the elders [also called overseers, and pastors] of the church that is a good thing. It is not a command that a tenth be given to the elders as though they replace the Levitical priesthood.

Deacons: The Stewardship of Church Resources Role

Originally the saints are reported to have brought their gifts to the apostles for distribution within the body in Acts 4. In Acts 6:1–6 we find that this was overwhelming their duties as teachers and that a role was created to help with this obligation within the body (later called Deacons in 1 Timothy 3:8–13). In many churches the role has been redefined, but we want to point out that when generous living intersects with the stewardship of church body resources, there's a biblical model for handling it.

Closing Thoughts

We're passionate about what God is doing inside of His body. We think it's really awesome that every saint throughout all of history was, is, or will be, getting to be part of the supernatural work that changes lives through stewardship. We pray that abiding in Christ and understanding will intersect in such a powerful way that you're energized and excited about your ability to reflect your life in Christ through the richness of His direction – and some of that might be through giving.

Stewardship covers a lot of area, it's about time, resources, money, and relationships. As you grow in your walk with the Lord He will likely expand your understanding of stewardship and the areas He will use you in. We hope you are significantly less concerned about percentages, and more concerned with spiritual intimacy with our God and one another.

The Ministries of the Holy Spirit[63]

By Dr. Bradley W. Maston

Introduction

The Holy Spirit is the third Person of the Trinity. The Holy Spirit is a Person – not an impersonal force or thing. He is in all ways God and shares in the Eternal essence of the Godhead. While the triune nature of the eternally existent godhead is beyond our ability to fully comprehend we can know and understand that each of the three persons of the Trinity (the Father, the Son, and The Holy Spirit) exist eternally and are separate in personality but united perfectly in essence. As such, each member of the trinity has different function in the universe as in eternity and each is important to understand as we live the Christian life. When we consider the ministries of the Holy Spirit we can consider what He does for unbelievers as well as for believers.

For Unbelievers

The unbeliever is dead in his trespasses and sins (Eph. 2:1). In the Bible "death" always carries the concept of separation. Thus, physical death is the separation from the material from the immaterial parts of man. It does not mean an inability to respond, but rather, separation. This the first and most important death that God promised would come should Adam and Eve disobey Him and eat from the Tree of the Knowledge of Good and Evil (Gen. 2:16-17). When Adam and Eve ate of that fruit their relationship with God was broken. Thus, spiritual life is defined by Jesus as knowing God through Jesus Christ (Jn. 17:3). The greatest need of the unbelieving person is to trust in Jesus and be saved by grace through faith. Thus,

[63] This short essay is based upon a greater study by Ron Merryman of Merryman Minsitries entitled *The Amazing Ministries of the Holy Spirit.* Find copies at merrymanministries.com.

the chief ministries of the Holy Spirit to the unbeliever are Conviction and Drawing.

The Convicting Ministry

> [8]And when He has come, **He will convict the world of sin**, and of righteousness, and of judgment: [9]of sin, because they do not believe in Me; [10]of righteousness, because I go to My Father and you see Me no more; [11]of judgment, because the ruler of this world is judged. (Jn. 16:8-11)

The convicting ministry of the Holy Spirit works in conjunction with their natural conscience to show the unbeliever that they have a need of God's forgiveness and righteousness.

The Drawing Ministry

> "And I, if I am lifted up from the earth, **will draw all peoples to Myself.**" (Jn. 12:32)

> I Jesus have sent mine angel to testify unto you these things in the churches. I am the root and the offspring of David, and the bright and morning star. **And the Spirit and the bride say, Come.** And let him that heareth say, Come. And let him that is athirst come. **And whosoever will, let him take the water of life freely.** (Rev 22:16–17)

The Holy Spirit is doing the work in the life of the unbeliever to draw and beckon that person towards Christ. So, we see that the Holy Spirit is working on the unbeliever to bring them to faith in Christ.

The Believer

The Holy Spirit is actively always working in every believer. The believer can only grow by walking by means of the Holy Spirit on a moment-by-moment basis (Gal. 5:16). While the ministries and work of the Holy Spirit are far greater than we are likely to understand in the scope of this earthly life, Ron Merryman has identified several important ministries of the Holy Spirit to the believer which are divided into the non-experiential ministries and the experiential ministries.

The Non-Experiential Ministries of the Holy Spirit to the Believer

The Non-Experiential Ministries of the Holy Spirit are so-called because they are true whether a believer feels them or senses them in any way. They are stated as a spiritually revealed fact in scripture. They are as follows:

- Regeneration – John 3:3,6; Titus 3:5
- Indwelling – 1 Corinthians 3:16; 6:19–20
- Baptizing – 1 Corinthians 12:13; Romans 6:3–5
- Sealing – Ephesians 1:13; 4:30; 2 Corinthians 1:22

Every believer is born again or regenerated by the power of the Holy Spirit. Every believer is also permanently indwelt by the Holy Spirit – making every believer the Temple of the Holy Spirit. The Baptism of the Holy Spirit has nothing to do with water baptism, but rather describes how every believer is immersed permanently in Christ, and thereafter always identified with Him. The sealing work of the Holy Spirit is the securing work of the Holy Spirit by which anyone who has trusted Christ is eternally secured and sealed into his or her eternal destiny in Christ.

The Experiential Ministries of the Holy Spirit

These important ministries of the Holy Spirit are the work of the Holy Spirit in the life of the believer. These ministries will be sensed by the believer in his everyday life. These ministries are the way in which God is working in the life of the Christian to bring growth and maturity. They are as follows:

- Comforting – John 14:16, 26
- Anointing – 1 John 2:20, 27

- Teaching – John 14:26; 1 John 2:27
- Assuring – Romans 8:16
- Guiding – Romans 8:14
- Interceding – Romans 8:26
- Convicting – John 16:7–11

There is no limit to the amount of time that could, and should, be invested in consideration of these remarkable ministries of the Holy Spirit in the Christian life. However, the brief explanation would simply be that God has given us His Son Jesus Christ, the Bible, the Church, and the Holy Spirit. In short, He has given us everything that we need for life and godliness (2 Pet. 1:3).

Conclusion

The Holy Spirit is working vitally and critically in the life of every person on earth to fulfill the plan of God for the Glory of God and by learning what He is doing we can most effectively co-operate with Him.

ALLIES UNAWARE?

A COMPARISON BETWEEN FREE GRACE AND TRADITIONAL BAPTIST SOTERIOLOGY

By J. Morgan Arnold

Introduction

For over half a millennium, many Christians in the West have self-identified as being either a Calvinist or an Arminian. However, in recent years, two theological camps, "Traditionalism" and "Free Grace," have established themselves as opponents to these long-standing philosophical systems. Both affirm that the concepts of God's sovereignty and man's libertarian free will, as related to soteriological matters, positively co-exist as important biblical doctrines. Traditionalists (also commonly known as "Provisionists") primarily comprise of members within the Southern Baptist Convention,[64] whereas "Free Gracers" typically attend many independent Bible churches and similar-minded evangelical churches.[65] Individuals within both of these camps have publicly and vociferously combated the growing influence of "Five-Point" Calvinism within evangelicalism. Thus, the question is posed: "How similar are the soteriological views of the two camps?" By understanding the roots of each group and investigating any theological commonalities and differences, a possible bridge could be built for Traditionalists and Free Gracers to engage in future opportunities for shared learning and edifying fellowship together.

---

[64] Eric Hankins, "A Statement of the Traditional Southern Baptist Understanding of God's Plan of Salvation," in *Anyone Can Be Saved: A Defense of "Traditional" Southern Baptist Soteriology*, ed. David L. Allen, Eric Hankins, and Adam Harwood (Eugene, OR: Wipf & Stock, 2016), 17.

[65] "Free Grace Church and Bible Study Tracker," Grace Evangelical Society, accessed July 9, 2021, https://faithalone.org/tracker/.

Definitions

What is Free Grace Soteriology

Free Grace soteriology, while not monolithic among proponents, is defined by Halsey:

> The Free Grace position maintains that salvation is by the grace of God through faith alone in Christ alone and not by works of any kind, such as commitment or surrender. The Free Grace position holds that salvation cannot come by a combination of grace and human effort. If grace could be maintained by human effort, then it ceases to be grace. Grace has no place for works, before, during or after salvation either to obtain it or keep it.[66]

Most Protestant soteriological systems espouse a belief in the five *solas* of the Reformation: *sola scriptura* (Scripture alone), *solus Christus* (Christ alone), *sola fide* (faith alone), *sola gratia* (grace alone), and *soli Deo gloria* (glory to God alone). Chay acknowledges, "All evangelicals would agree that we are 'saved by faith alone.'"[67] However, Free Grace Theology indignantly defines "faith alone" as, truly, faith *alone.* Proponents of Free Grace biblically support their premise by pointing to Eph. 2:8–9: "For by grace you have been saved through faith; and this is not of yourselves, it is the gift of God; not a result of works, so that no one may boast." Of this passage, Anderson remarks, "…Paul qualifies grace by saying it is a *free gift.* A free gift has no strings attached on the front end (or it becomes a wage) and no strings attached on the back end (or it is a bribe)."[68]

---

[66] Michael D. Halsey, "What is Free Grace Theology?" in *Freely By His Grace: Classical Grace Theology*, ed. J.B. Hixson, Rick Whitmire, and Roy B. Zuck (Duluth, MN: Grace Gospel Press, 2012), 7.

[67] Fred Chay, ed., *A Defense of Free Grace Theology: With Respect to Saving Faith, Perseverance, and Assurance* (The Woodlands, TX: Grace Theology Press, 2017), 2.

[68] David Anderson, *Free Grace Soteriology*, 3rd ed. (The Woodlands, TX: Grace Theology Press, 2018), xii.

What is Traditional Baptist Soteriology

Traditional Baptist soteriology, also referred to as Traditionalism (and becoming more prominently known in recent years as Provisionalism),[69] is defined by Hankins as being "grounded in the conviction that every person can and must be saved by a personal and free decision to respond to the gospel by trusting in Christ Jesus alone as Savior and Lord."[70] Hankins' defining document for Traditionalism, "A Statement of the Traditional Southern Baptist Understanding of God's Plan of Salvation", was admittedly birthed into existence as a counter-offensive measure:

> The precipitating issue for this statement is the rise of a movement called New Calvinism among Southern Baptists. This movement is committed to advancing in the churches an exclusively Calvinistic understanding of salvation, characterized by an aggressive insistence on the "doctrines of grace" (TULIP), and to the goal of making Calvinism the central Southern Baptist position on God's plan of salvation.[71]

Origins

Both Free Gracers and Traditionalists claim their general theological concepts extend back to the writings of the Apostles. In the Modern Era, both groups also trace a specific lineage of writings and adherents for their definitive positions back to the mid-nineteenth century. Chay writes, "There is a vast field of literature that advocates for and promotes a Free Grace theological perspective predating

---

[69] Leighton Flowers, "*Labels: Traditionalism vs PROVISIONALISM,*" YouTube video, 17:25, Soteriology 101, September 28, 2017, https://www.youtube.com/watch?v=A9HAQxWwhJA, 0:52. It was Leighton Flowers who first coined the terms "Provisionalism" and "Provisionists" to better describe the Traditionalist view held by that God has made provision for all people the ability to be saved through belief in His Son Jesus Christ.

[70] Hankins, *Anyone Can Be Saved*, 17.

[71] Ibid., 16.

(Zane) Hodges (1970s). Robert Govett (1860s) was a fellow at the University of Oxford who wrote voluminous exegetical and theological works advocating Free Grace interpretations."[72] Chay also mentions the Free Grace writings of George H. Peters, Alexander Peterson, and G.H. Pember in the late 1800s, and D.M. Panton, Watchman Nee, G.H. Lang, and R.E. Neighbor in the early 1900s, not to mention the influential Lewis Sperry Chafer who "taught much of a Free Grace perspective in general, if not in every nuance of the view."[73]

On the Traditionalist side, Lemke, in his historical research of the Southern Baptist Convention discovered that,

> in the first seventy-five years of the Southern Baptist Convention (1845-1920): (a) while affirmed by some churches and associations, five-point Calvinism was not dominant among most Baptist churches in the South after the Second Great Awakening, (b) actual churches and associations reflected a broader diversity than any one view, and (c) most characteristic was a distinctively Baptist hybrid mixture of Calvinism and Arminianism that fell short of an affirmation of either five-point Calvinism or five-point Arminianism.... (M)ost Southern Baptists since the inception of our convention are neither fully Calvinist nor Arminian, but a unique and distinct Baptist tradition that is somewhere between these two extremes.[74]

Such historical evidence should put to rest any criticism that Free Grace theology and Traditional Southern Baptist soteriology are only recent constructs and should be discounted from serious theological consideration because of their "youth."

---

[72] Chay, *A Defense of Free Grace Theology*, 21-22.

[73] Ibid., 22.

[74] Steve W. Lemke, "History or Revisionist History? How Calvinistic Were the Overwhelming Majority of Baptists and Their Confessions in the South until the Twentieth Century?," *Southwestern Journal of Theology* 57, no. 2 (Spring 2015): 242-243.

Development of the Free Grace Movement

Free Grace theology was primarily articulated and nuanced by leaders and professors at Dallas Theological Seminary in the latter half of the 20th century. Prominent theologians in this group included John Walvoord, J. Dwight Pentecost, Howard Hendricks, Roy Zuck, Charles Ryrie, and Zane Hodges.[75] Popular Free Grace pastors had influential international radio ministries starting in the 1960s (J. Vernon McGee), 1970s (Charles Stanley and Chuck Swindoll), and 1980s (Tony Evans). In 1986, Bob Wilkin, a disciple of Hodge, founded the Grace Evangelical Society (GES). GES helped spread the Free Grace message through conferences, debates, books, and *The Journal of the Grace Evangelical Society* which became a semi-annual publication. In 2004, the Free Grace Alliance was birthed by Charlie Bing, Fred Lybrand, and Earl Radmacher for the purpose of connecting Free Grace ministries and advancing Free Grace concepts around the world. Today, the Free Grace Movement continues to promote the "justification by faith alone apart from any works" message to a new generation through Bible colleges and seminaries, conferences, books, websites, radio broadcasts, videos, and podcasts.

Development of SBC Traditional Soteriology

In the 20th century, "the primary confessor of each version of The Baptist Faith and Message (E.Y. Mullins in 1925, Herschel Hobbs in 1963, and Adrian Rogers in 2000) uniformly held to the view of salvation that is described in the Traditional Statement."[76] As the Southern Baptist Convention moved into the 21st century, Fisher Humphreys and Paul Robertson, professors at New Orleans Baptist Theological Seminary, popularized the "Traditional Baptist" moniker when they wrote *God So Loved the World: Traditional Baptists and Calvinism*

---

[75] Chay, *A Defense of Free Grace Theology*, 22.

[76] Leighton Flowers, "The Rise of Soteriological Traditionalism," Soteriology101, October 10, 2016, https://soteriology101.com/2016/10/10/the-rise-of-soteriological-traditionalism/.

in 2001. In 2008, Jerry Vines organized the *John 3:16 Conference* in Lawrenceville, GA, in direct response to the growing Calvinist movement within the SBC. In 2012, Eric Hankins, a pastor from Mississippi, authored a soteriological statement named *A Statement of the Traditional Southern Baptist Understanding of God's Plan of Salvation* (Traditional Statement). It served as a "shot across the bow" to the growing encroachment of the Calvinist armada within the SBC. In 2013, a group named *Connect 316* was formed "to counter Calvinist groups such as the Founders Conference, Acts 29, 9Marks, The Gospel Coalition, and Together for the Gospel gaining influence in the Southern Baptist Convention and other Conservative Evangelical Groups[77] (unfortunately Connect 316 disbanded in 2019). In 2014, Leighton Flowers[78], a former Five-Point Calvinist pastor, created a YouTube channel, podcast, and website named *Soteriology 101* which spoke out against Calvinism and promoted the Traditionalist view. Then, in 2016, a group of influential Traditionalist pastors including Eric and David Hankins, David Allen, Adam Harwood, Steve Lemke, and Ronnie Rogers collaborated to write *Anyone Can Be Saved: A Defense of "Traditional" Southern Baptist Soteriology*. Today, while more Traditionalist voices are being heard online, there is not a prominent annual gathering of Traditionalists occurring either at the SBC's Annual Meeting or as an organized independent conference.

Commonalities

A Common "Opponent" (New Calvinism)

Both Free Gracers and Traditionalists have constantly been forced to defend their positions against harsh criticism levelled against them by Reformed theologians and pastors. The book *A Defense of Free Grace Theology: With Respect to Saving Faith, Perseverance, and Assurance,*

---

[77] Leighton Flowers, "The Rise of Soteriological Traditionalism." Soteriology101. October 10, 2016. https://baptistnews.com/article/traditionalist-blog-sbc-today-says-goodbye/#.YPy40o5KhPY

[78] Chay, preface to *A Defense of Free Grace Theology*.

edited by Chay, is primarily a rebuttal to Reformed theologian Wayne Grudem's 2016 book *Free Grace Theology: 5 Ways It Diminishes the Gospel.*[15] Chay contends that Grudem's book "describes the Free Grace gospel as being a 'weakened' message, a 'watered down' message, and a 'diminished gospel', as the title of the book describes."[79]

Similarly, the book *Anyone Can Be Saved: A Defense of "Traditional" Southern Baptist Soteriology*, edited by Allen, Hankins, and Harwood, is a response to attacks made from both Calvinist and Arminian leaders upon the Traditional Statement. Both Albert Mohler,[80] a Reformed seminary president, and Roger Olsen,[81] an American Baptist professor of the Arminian persuasion, erroneously accuse the Traditional Statement of being "semi-Pelagian." According to *The Oxford Dictionary of the Christian Church*, semi-Pelagians "maintained that the first steps towards the Christian life were ordinarily taken by the human will and that grace supervened only later."[82] Harwood refutes this label by citing three instances listed within the Traditional Statement which clearly articulate that God is the initiator in the salvific process.[83] This is just one of many examples in which the Traditional Statement has been maligned, mischaracterized, and misunderstood by its theological opponents on both ends of the soteriological spectrum.

Recently, both Free Gracers and Provisionists have become more polemic in their battle against Reformed theology. This is evidenced by

---

[79] Ibid., 12.

[80] Adam Harwood, "Is the Traditional Statement Semi-Pelagian?" in *Anyone Can Be Saved: A Defense of "Traditional" Southern Baptist Soteriology*, ed. David L. Allen, Eric Hankins, and Adam Harwood (Eugene, OR: Wipf & Stock, 2016), 167.

[81] Ibid., 163–67

[82] F.L. Cross and E.A. Livingstone, eds., *The Oxford Dictionary of the Christian Church*, 3rd ed. (Oxford: Oxford University Press, 2005), s.v. "Semi-pelagianism"

[83] Harwood, *Anyone Can Be Saved*, 160.

a number of books[84], videos, and podcasts[85] questioning Calvinism. Both camps are effectively taking the fight to Reformed soteriology.

Commonalities in Soteriology

In addition to Provisionists and Free Gracers having a common theological opponent, the two also share many similar theological positions. However, neither camp is theologically monolithic on every jot and tittle.[86]

Statements found in the Traditional Statement for which most Free Grace proponents would agree upon include:

- The message of the Gospel: "The Gospel is the good news that God has made a way of salvation through the life, death, and resurrection of the Lord Jesus Christ for any person. This is in keeping with God's desire for every person to be saved. We deny that only a select few are capable of responding to the gospel while the rest are predestined to an eternity in hell (Article One)."[87]
- The problem of man's sinfulness: "Because of the fall of Adam, every person inherits a nature and environment inclined toward sin and that every person who is capable of moral action will sin. Each person's sin alone brings the wrath

---

[84] Recent examples of books criticizing Calvinism included *Is Calvinism Biblical? Let The Scriptures Decide* by Robert Wilkin, *Confronting Calvinism* by Anthony Badger, *The Extent of the Atonement: A Historical and Critical Review* by David L. Allen, and *Reflections of a Disenchanted Calvinist: The Disquieting Realities of Calvinism* by Ronnie W. Rogers.

[85] Some podcasts which have questioned the claims of Calvinism include "Soteriology 101" by Leighton Flowers, "Beyond the Fundamentals" by Kevin Thompson, and "Grace In Focus Radio" by Grace Evangelical Society.

[86] For an assessment of doctrinal commonalities and differences the following resources will be utilized: *A Statement of the Traditional Southern Baptist Understanding of God's Plan of Salvation* (Traditional Statement), the Baptist Faith & Message 2000, the Covenant for the Free Grace Alliance, and content found in the book *Freely By His Grace: Classical Grace Theology.*

[87] Ibid., 19.

of a holy God, broken fellowship with Him, ever-worsening selfishness and destructiveness, death, and condemnation to an eternity in hell. We deny that Adam's sin resulted in the incapacitation of any person's free will... While no sinner is remotely capable of achieving salvation through his own effort, we deny that any sinner is saved apart from a free response to the Holy Spirit's drawing through the Gospel (Article Two)." [88]

- The unlimited atonement of Christ: "We affirm that the penal substitution of Christ is the only available and effective sacrifice for the sins of every person.... We deny that God imposes or withholds this atonement without respect to an act of the person's free will. We deny that Christ died only for the sins of those who will be saved (Article Three)."[89]
- The grace of God provides salvation for any person by taking all of the initiative in providing atonement, in freely offering the Gospel in the power of the Holy Spirit, and in uniting the believer to Christ through the Holy Spirit by faith. We deny that grace negates the necessity of a free response of faith or that it cannot be resisted. We deny that the response of faith is in any way a meritorious work that earns salvation (Article Four)."[90]
- The necessity for the sinner to "respond to the Gospel and become born again through the power of the Holy Spirit. The sinner becomes a new creation in Christ and enters, at the moment he believes, into eternal life. We deny that any person is regenerated prior to or apart from hearing and responding to the Gospel (Article Five)."[91]

---

[88] Ibid.

[89] Ibid., 20.

[90] Ibid.

[91] Ibid., 20-21

- Denial of double predestination: "We deny that election means that, from eternity, God predestined certain people for salvation and others for condemnation (Article Six)."[92]
- The sovereignty of God: "We affirm God's eternal knowledge of and sovereignty over every person's salvation or condemnation. We deny that God's sovereignty and knowledge require Him to cause a person's acceptance or rejection of faith in Christ (Article Seven)."[93]
- The free will of man: "We affirm that God, as an expression of His sovereignty, endows each person with actual free will (the ability to choose between two options), which must be exercised in accepting or rejecting God's gracious call to salvation by the Holy Spirit... We deny that the decision of faith is an act of God rather than a response of the person. We deny there is an 'effectual call' for certain people different from a 'general call' to any person who hears and understands the Gospel (Article Eight)." [94]
- The security of the believer: "When a person responds in faith to the Gospel, God promises to complete the process of salvation in the believer into eternity. This process begins with justification, whereby the sinner is immediately acquitted of all sin…; continues in sanctification, whereby the saved are progressively conformed to the image of Christ by the indwelling Holy Spirit; and concludes in glorification, whereby the saint enjoys life with Christ in heaven forever. We deny that this Holy Spirit-sealed relationship can ever be broken (Article Nine)."[95]
- The Great Commission: "The Lord Jesus Christ commissioned His church to preach the good news of salvation to all people to the ends of the earth. We affirm the proclamation of the Gospel is God's means of bringing any

[92] Ibid., 21

[93] Ibid.

[94] Ibid., 22.

[95] Ibid.

> person to salvation. We deny that salvation is possible outside of a faith response to the Gospel of Jesus Christ (Article Ten)."[96]

Commonalities in Other Doctrines and Issues

Proponents of Traditional Southern Baptist and Free Grace soteriologies both affirm basic Christian beliefs found in the Apostles' and Nicene Creeds. In addition, areas in which most Free Gracers would be in agreement with the Baptist Faith & Message 2000 include:

- The Bible is the inspired, inerrant, and infallible Word of God.
- Pastors and elders are to be men.
- Only two ordinances observed by the church: baptism and the Lord's Supper.
- The future consummation of the Kingdom of God after the return of Christ.
- The eternal punishment of the unregenerate in a literal hell.

In addition, SBC Traditionalism and the Free Grace movement share the same views on the divine institution of marriage (the commitment between one man and one woman), the headship of the husband, the importance of the divine institution of family, the belief that human life begins at conception, and the recognition of the divine institution of civil government. While not unified in their eschatological views, many (if not most) Southern Baptists would agree with the Free Grace positions of classical dispensationalism, a pretribulation-premillennial rapture of the Church, a literal seven-year tribulation period, a literal physical return of Christ, and a literal thousand-year reign of Christ on earth followed by the Eternal Kingdom.

---

[96] Ibid, 23.

Commonalities in Purpose

Both Provisionists and Free Gracers share the common goal of Jesus' Great Commission: "Go therefore and make disciples of all the nations, baptizing them in the name of the Father and the Son and the Holy Spirit, teaching them to observe all that I commanded you; and lo, I am with you always, even to the end of the age" (Mt. 28:19-20). Southern Baptists have vibrantly heeded this call since their inception. Statistics report that there are over 10,000 SBC missionaries serving within the U.S. and around the world.[97] Likewise, the Free Grace movement has actively sent leaders, teachers and missionaries to locations around the globe. Proponents of Free Grace theology have been instrumental in many international missions organizations including Central American Mission International, New Tribes Mission, GoodSeed International, Village Ministries International, Disciple Makers Multiplied, Evantell, East West Ministries, and AWANA.[98]

Differences

Despite the many doctrines and beliefs shared by Provisionists and Free Gracers there are still at least three prominent issues deserving of further clarification and dialogue between the two parties. These three issues include the roles that (1) lordship and (2) repentance play at the point of justification for new believers, and (3) whether a believer can ever commit apostasy.

The Role of Lordship in Justification

One of the most highly debated subjects within the Christian faith over the past half-century is what has been labeled "lordship salvation." Gentry, a Reformed theologian, writes: "The Lordship view

---

[97] Hankins, Anyone Can Be Saved, 9.

[98] Bret Nazworth, "God's Grace in Missions, Evangelism, and Disciple-Making," in *Freely By His Grace: Classical Grace Theology*, ed. J.B. Hixson, Rick Whitmire, and Roy B. Zuck (Duluth, MN: Grace Gospel Press, 2012), 554.

expressly states the need to acknowledge Christ as the Lord and Master of one's life in the act of truly receiving Him as Savior. These are not two different, sequential acts (or successive steps), but rather one act of pure trusting faith."[99] Bing, a Free Grace theologian, says that though there are theological variances, mostly all advocates of lordship salvation believe, "The gospel message includes a call to surrender to the lordship of Jesus Christ and a decision to submit to Him as Master of all of one's life."[100]

In the Preamble of the Traditional Statement, Hankins writes, "Traditional Southern Baptist soteriology is grounded in the conviction that every person can and must be saved by a personal and free decision to respond to the Gospel by trusting in Christ Jesus alone as Savior *and Lord* ."[101] This belief by the SBC is further confirmed by the Baptist Faith & Message 2000 which states: "Faith is the acceptance of Jesus Christ and commitment of the entire personality to Him as *Lord* and Saviour."[102]

For years, the Free Grace camp has vociferously countered such wording found in the aforementioned Baptist documents. The battle lines for the modern debate were drawn after Zane Hodges' book *The Gospel Under Siege* (1981) exposed the fallacies of lordship salvation, and found itself under siege by John MacArthur, Jr.'s best seller *The Gospel According to Jesus (1988).* In response to MacArthur's book, several Free Grace books were written the following year including Charles Ryrie's *So Great Salvation* and a follow-up book by Hodges, *Absolutely Free.*

One of the reasons why Free Grace is passionately opposed to the teaching of lordship salvation is due to the soteriological belief that

---

[99] Kenneth L. Gentry, *Lord of the Saved* (Phillipsburg, NJ: Presbyterian and Reformed, 1992), 10.

[100] Charles C. Bing, "What About Lordship Salvation?" in *Freely By His Grace: Classical Grace Theology*, ed. J.B. Hixson, Rick Whitmire, and Roy B. Zuck (Duluth, MN: Grace Gospel Press, 2012), 554.

[101] Hankins, Anyone Can Be Saved, 17 [emphasis added].

[102] Southern Baptist Convention, "Baptist Faith & Message 2000," May 18, 2020, https://bfm.sbc.net /bfm2000_[emphasis added].

there is a distinct difference between a Christian's justification, the moment in time in which a person believes in Jesus and is counted as righteous in the sight of God, and a Christian's sanctification, his daily walk with Christ occurs *after* justification. Lybrand points out, pastors and theologians encounter a dilemma when this biblical concept is either ignored or not understood: "The blurring of the distinction between faith in Christ and following Christ inevitably leads down a trail away from grace and back to works."[103] Proponents of lordship salvation will shout "*Sola fide*" ("Faith alone") with gusto from the mountaintops, but when their theology is closely investigated, it is discovered that such proclamations do not meet eye-to-eye with their actual belief system. In Acts 16:31, the Philippian jailer asked Paul and Silas, "Sirs, what must I do to be saved?" Their response was simple: "Believe in the Lord Jesus, and you will be saved, you and your household." Unfortunately, in diametric opposition to Paul and Silas' answer, the lordship camp tacks on any number of additional requirements for justification: "pick up your cross", "forsake yourself", "repent of all of your sins", "surrender all", "give up all for the kingdom", "completely resign your old self", "submit absolutely", "commit fully", etc. Such statements are to be marks of a growing Christian as he or she matures in his daily walk with Christ (sanctification), but an unregenerate person, or even a newborn babe in Christ, is not going to be able to fully comprehend the meaning of these concepts.

Free Grace writings have always embraced the doctrine of the lordship of Christ. Free Grace theology strongly advocates that all Christians should walk daily in Christ with the understanding that Jesus is Lord over all aspects of their lives. However, while opposing the unreasonable commands of lordship salvation, Free Grace heartily promotes the biblical concept of lordship *sanctification*. Thus, any lordship mandates at the point of justification from the Provisionist camp would be a sticking point with Free Gracers.

---

[103] Fred R. Lybrand, "The Distinction between Salvation and Discipleship," in *Freely By His Grace: Classical Grace Theology*, ed. J.B. Hixson, Rick Whitmire, and Roy B. Zuck (Duluth, MN: Grace Gospel Press, 2012), 136.

The Role of Repentance in Justification

Closely related to the concept of lordship salvation is the view that repentance must be included with faith when an unregenerate person receives the free gift of salvation. The Southern Baptist Traditional Statement mentions the necessity of repentance *and* faith three times:

- under Article Three: The Atonement of Christ: "We deny that this atonement results in salvation without a person's free response of repentance and faith."[104]
- under Article Five: The Regeneration of the Sinner: "We affirm that any person who responds to the gospel with repentance and faith is born again through the power of the Holy Spirit."[105]
- under Article Six: Election to Salvation: "We affirm that, in reference to salvation, election speaks of God's eternal, gracious, and certain plan in Christ to have a people who are his by repentance and faith."[106]

Similarly, The Baptist Faith & Message 2000 states, "Justification is God's gracious and full acquittal upon principles of His righteousness of all sinners who repent and believe in Christ."[107] Many in the Free Grace camp would concur that repentance *must* be coupled with faith during justification.[108] However, the reason they hold this view is because their definition of repentance, in light of justification, is not considered a work such as "reformation", "penance", "expressing godly sorrow", "actively turning from sins", or "total

---

[104] Hankins, *Anyone Can Be Saved*, 20.

[105] Ibid.

[106] Hankins, *Anyone Can Be Saved*, 21.

[107] Southern Baptist Convention, "Baptist Faith & Message 2000."

[108] Richard A. Seymour, "Repentance and the Free Gift of God," in *Freely By His Grace: Classical Grace Theology*, ed. J.B. Hixson, Rick Whitmire, and Roy B. Zuck (Duluth, MN: Grace Gospel Press, 2012), 196.

surrender."[109] Rather, the most common Free Grace definition is that repentance is a "change of mind" or a "change of thinking". Chafer puts it this way: "repentance, which is a change of mind, is included in believing. No individual can turn to Christ from some other confidence without a change of mind."[110] Ryrie agrees:

> *There is a repentance that is unto eternal salvation.* What kind of repentance saves? Not a sorrow that results in a cleaning up of one's life. People who reform have repented; that is, they have changed their minds about their past lives, but that kind of repentance, albeit genuine, does not save them. The only kind of repentance that saves anyone, anywhere, anytime is a change of mind about Jesus Christ. The sense of sin and sorrow because of sin may stir up a person's mind or conscience so that he or she realized the need for a Savior, but if there is not change of mind about Jesus Christ there will be no salvation.[111]

So, could it be, as often is the case in theology, that any differences between the two camps on the issue of repentance are purely semantical? Does the SBC's definition of repentance indeed line up with Free Grace theology? Unfortunately, the answer is no. The Baptist Faith & Message 2000 states "Repentance is a *genuine* turning from sin toward God."[112] In other words, repentance is an act that a person must do to become a believer in Christ. Thus, the definition of repentance and the salvific role it plays in justification, the "first tense of salvation," would be a sticking point between Traditionalists and Free Gracers.

---

[109] Ibid., 204-210.

[110] Lewis Sperry Chafer, *Systematic Theology*, vol. 3 (Grand Rapids, MI: Kregel, 1993), 374.

[111] Charles C. Ryrie, *So Great Salvation: What It Means to Believe in Jesus Christ* (Chicago: Moody, 1997), 85.

[112] Southern Baptist Convention, "Baptist Faith & Message 2000, IV. Salvation [emphasis added]."

The Possibility of Apostasy in Sanctification

Another concept that is housed under the umbrella of lordship salvation concerns the belief that a "true Christian" could never commit apostasy and abandon the faith. In Free Grace theology, while the sin of apostasy by a believer is repugnant, it is still a sin which was paid for by Jesus' atonement upon the cross. Since neither Free Gracers nor Provisionists would classify apostasy as the "unpardonable sin," then apostasy must be considered a sin that is pardonable. However, that is not what mainstream Baptist theology teaches.

Article Nine of the *Traditional Statement* says, "We deny that this Holy Spirit-sealed relationship can ever be broken." Free Gracers would heartily say "Amen" to that but would savagely oppose the caveat contained in the next sentence: "We *deny* even the possibility of apostasy."[113] In the minds of Traditionalists, if someone committed the sin of apostasy, they must have never been a Christian in the first place. In rebuttal, Dillow makes an excellent observation:

> If the Bible offers illustrations of regenerate individuals who have persisted in sin for a lengthy period and finished life as failures before God, the [Calvinist] theory of the saint's perseverance is simply wrong. No amount of special pleading that these are simply "descriptions of the failure of one man" rather than the "teaching of Scripture" will do. If one man who is born again fails to persevere in holiness, then the Scriptures cannot teach that all who are born again will "*continue in the Christian life*" and "*persevere until the end of their lives.*"[114]

Dillow gives Old Testament and New Testament examples of people who did not finish their lives strong in the faith: Rehoboam,

---

[113] Hankins, *Anyone Can Be Saved*, 22.

[114] Joseph Dillow, "The Possibility of Failure in the Christian Life," in *A Defense of Free Grace Theology: With Respect to Saving Faith, Perseverance, and Assurance*, ed. Fred Chay (The Woodlands, TX: Grace Theology Press, 2017), 281.

Jehu, Joash, Uzziah, Saul, Asa, Solomon, Simon Magus, Hymenaeus, Alexander, and Demas. Thus, the denial of even the possibility of an apostate being regenerate would be a sticking point between Provisionists and Free Gracers.

The Future

Admittedly, there are definite points of soteriological contention between Free Grace and Traditionalism. Thankfully, the doctrinal similarities outnumber the differences. It is important to remember that while Free Gracers have primarily been battling lordship salvation arguments for the past half century, Traditional Southern Baptists have not only had to combat an encroaching neo-Calvinism, but they have also had to passionately fight for the heart and soul of their denomination against liberal theology and claims of biblical errancy.

Recent statistics show that the SBC is comprised of 15 million members, making it easily the largest Protestant denomination in the United States.[115] In a personal interview this author conducted with Dr. David L. Allen, former Distinguished Professor of Preaching at Southwestern Baptist Theological Seminary, Dr. Allen relayed that while 40-50% of SBC pastors consider themselves Calvinist, roughly only 10-20% of SBC laypeople agree with Five-Point Calvinism.[116] Dr. Allen said he honestly felt that Neo-Calvinism was very close to hitting a glass ceiling.

A growing number of SBC leaders and laypeople are seeking to educate and arm themselves concerning Calvinism. In doing so, they will undoubtedly discover the absence of grace within the "doctrines of grace." Many will learn of lordship salvation's laborious requirements and lack of salvific assurance. At this point, it will be

---

[115] Hankins, *Anyone Can Be Saved*, 9.

[116] David L. Allen, interview by author, Denton, TX, July 15, 2021. Dr. Allen has been a shining example of how Provisionists and Free Gracers can work together. He has written reviews and endorsements promoting Free Grace books. He has also given a commencement address for Grace School of Theology, a Free Grace seminary in The Woodlands, TX.

interesting to discover how many will become more aware of and attracted to the biblical truths found within Free Grace theology.

In the meantime, there is still much work to do to sufficiently get the message of Free Grace theology into the marketplace of ideas so it can enjoy its day in the court of public opinion. Future dialogue between Free Grace and Traditionalist leaders can serve to knock down any straw man arguments and false understandings. With the disbandment of the Connect 316 conference, Traditionalist pastors, at the time of this writing, do not have an annual or regional conference to attend in which they can discuss their shared ideas and values. Now might be the perfect time for the Free Grace Movement to reach out to these pastors and invite them to attend any number of Free Grace conferences and seminars which are held around the country. Now might be the perfect time to enlighten any Baptist leaders and laypeople who are under the impression that Free Grace theology equates to "easy believism", "cheap grace", "non-lordship", antinomianism, and a departure from historic evangelical Christianity. Now might be the perfect time for Christians in both camps who love God's Word to come together as allies and engage in meaningful times of honest discussion, shared learning, and authentic fellowship under the banner of grace.

BIBLIOGRAPHY

Allen, David L., Eric Hankins, and Adam Harwood, eds. *Anyone Can Be Saved: A Defense of "Traditional" Southern Baptist Soteriology.* Eugene, OR: Wipf & Stock, 2016.

Anderson, David R. *Free Grace Soteriology.* 3rd ed. The Woodlands, TX: Grace Theology Press, 2018.

Chafer, L. S. *Systematic Theology*, vol. 3. Grand Rapids, MI: Kregel, 1993.

Chay, Fred, ed. *A Defense of Free Grace Theology: With Respect to Saving Faith, Perseverance, and Assurance.* The Woodlands, TX: Grace Theology Press, 2017.

Cross, F. L. *The Oxford Dictionary of the Christian Church.* 3rd ed. E. A. Livingstone, ed. Oxford: Oxford University Press, 2005. s.v. "Semi-pelagianism."

Flowers, Leighton. *God's Provision for All: A Defense of God's Goodness.* Coppell, TX: Trinity Academic Press, 2019.

———. "Labels: Traditionalism vs PROVISIONALISM." Soteriology 101. YouTube video, 17:25. September 28, 2017, https://www.youtube.com/watch?v=A9HAQxWwhJA.

———. "The Rise of Soteriological Traditionalism." Soteriology 101. October 10, 2016. https://soteriology101.com/2016/10/10/the-rise-of-soteriological-traditionalism/.

Gentry, Kenneth L. *Lord of the Saved.* Phillipsburg, NJ: Presbyterian and Reformed, 1992.

Grace Evangelical Society. "Free Grace Church and Bible Study Tracker." Accessed July 9, 2021. https://faithalone.org/tracker

Hixson, J.B., Rick Whitmire, and Roy B. Zuck, eds. *Freely By His Grace: Classical Grace Theology.* Duluth, MN: Grace Gospel Press, 2012.

Hodges, Zane C. *Absolutely Free: A Biblical Reply to Lordship Salvation.* 2nd ed. Corinth, TX: Grace Evangelical Society, 2014.

Lemke, Steve W. "History or Revisionist History? How Calvinistic Were the Overwhelming Majority of Baptists and Their Confessions in the South until the Twentieth Century?" *Southwestern Journal of Theology* 57, no. 2 (Spring 2015): 242-243.

Ryrie, Charles C. *So Great Salvation: What It Means to Believe in Jesus Christ.* Chicago: Moody, 1997.

Southern Baptist Convention. "Baptist Faith & Message 2000." May 18, 2020. https://bfm.sbc.net/bfm2000.

The Value and Importance of the Old Testament Pseudepigrapha

Dr. Bradley W. Maston

> What advantage then has the Jew, or what is the profit of circumcision? Much in every way! Chiefly because to them were committed the oracles of God. (Rom. 3:1–2)

Statement of Purpose: The Pseudepigrapha is of critical value

For many Evangelical Christians today the Pseudepigrapha is entirely unknown, and to those who are familiar the Pseudepigrapha of the Old Testament is treated with a high degree of caution or even distain. Sadly, this trend is not unwarranted. For the liberal scholar and the critic of the Bible the Pseudepigrapha is often used as a base camp to substantiate doubts and attacks upon the uniqueness and reliability of Scripture. As this paper will show those attacks are wholly unsubstantiated as there is no logical reason to question the authenticity of the Biblical texts simply due to similarity with extra-biblical texts. On the contrary, the similarity strengthens and substantiates our understanding of the reliability, uniqueness, and authenticity of Scripture. Thus, the purpose of this short paper is to give the reader a bit of background on the Pseudepigrapha and its usefulness to today's Bible student.

A Definition of the Pseudepigrapha

One of the challenges that surrounds this body of literature is the very name Pseudepigrapha. The name itself tells us that these documents have been written and attributed to people who did not write them. There is a great difficulty in this. The truth is that most of the works we simply do not know whether who wrote them…or whether they are authentic. However, their inauthenticity is not a foregone conclusion.

Other Possible Interpretations

It has already been mentioned that this is not a unified corpus of literature, like the Scriptures. They are books that were written, passed down, scattered, and collected over the years. This means that the merits of each must be measured individually. This brings the point of considering each of these works. As has been said, they cannot be considered as a group, but must be considered individually. Thus, we must entertain the options which are available in considering these works. I would like to consider a 4 major options, realizing that any given work of the Pseudepigrapha may well fall into all five categories!

1. *They are perfectly genuine* – The prescribed author could be genuine, in whole or in part. Israel had a tremendous and powerful literary tradition. The reality that the entire faith was contained and communicated through the written Torah meant that there would be a large literate community always around…ready to read, write, and preserve literary works from generation to generation.
2. *They are malicious lies* – The next logical possibility is that they are malicious lies. Some of these books may have been written under demonic influence, and others by people who had a specific agenda that they wished to pedal.
3. *The work of lunatics* –There is no doubt that mental instability can bring about all sorts of religious delusion. Again, the possibility of demonic possession must also be considered in this option. It is possible that many of these works were written or influenced heavily by those who are mentally unstable and thus believed what they were writing to be revealed by God but were the result of mental illness.
4. *They are fictions written by unknown authors to make sense of history* – This option is favored by many secular academics and is utilized with a particular agenda of trying to delegitimize the clear predictive accuracy of the Bible…most specifically the prophetic accuracy of Daniel. The thrust of this theory is that those who considered their history, in a desire to make sense of it would write their history as a prophetic symbolic work to highlight the plan of God.

Any of these four options may be the case for these works, or, more likely, some combination of the four. We must also understand that these works were not under the protective and guiding hand of God and may have been handed down, reworked, and changed significantly from their original forms. While we may not be able to come to our conclusions with dogmatic certainty we can certainly understand and evaluate these various options as we would any other non-biblical text of any period. These books will contain truth, error, accuracy, and inaccuracy. Just as we would assume when we read the more recognized works of Josephus, Herodotus, and the Church Fathers.

Important Points - Uses

The fact that these works are not, and never were, considered a part of the canon of Scripture is of the utmost importance. There can be no serious case made that any of these works would be in any way the "*lost books of the Bible.*" The Bible, by its very nature and character cannot have lost because it was God himself who guided the process of their writing, preservation, and recognition as the authoritative word of God. The ridiculous claim that there could be a "lost book" of the Bible is generally an attack by those secularists who do not believe that the Bible is a supernatural book to begin with. Meaning that they are fallaciously using the term "Bible" on both sides of the equation as fits their anti-supernatural bias but with an utter lack of logical consistency. Nevertheless, it is important to be very clear…these books are not Scripture, nor are they on par with Scripture, nor (with only a few exceptions) have they been viewed as scripture by any group of believers in Church History. (Enoch and the Catholic Apocrypha being the only notable exceptions to the last point).

Once we have made the clear designation that these books are not on par with Scripture we are free to treat them as we would treat any original source. It is not impossible that the Lord would have revealed things to certain individuals and chosen not to enshrine them in the Bible. Certainly, we would read the salvation experiences of the great saints of past and present alike and say with all confidence that while their accounts do not belong in scripture that they are valid and profitable examples of all that the Lord has done in their lives and might to in the lives of any who will trust in Jesus Christ. Thus, it is no threat at all to the trustworthiness of the Bible to think that the Lord may have given some other believer in history a divine vision of the future, or brought them up in to heaven as with Isaiah. We must, of course be extraordinarily cautious, and not allow their accounts to be authoritative, but a survey of this type of literature will prove that many of these encounters and experiences in no way contradict the Biblical record…but rather affirm its accuracy.

Apart from this we find that even if every word of these works were patently false they give us great insight into the literary heritage and background to the Bible. This provides us with a larger cultural context and ability to interpret and respond to the various figures of speech and usage of various words and contexts that we may never have apart from these works. Clearly, these works are worthy of consideration. It is particularly important at this point in history, when the widespread availability of the information allows us to dig deeper into the information that previous generations could only hope to rely upon the far off advice of some "expert" whose reputation could be trusted.

Conclusion

The so called Pseudepigrapha is of great value to the Bible student. With the right perspective we find that it provides a confirmation of the high standard of the canon of Scripture, the consistency of the understanding of the Scripture down through History, and the right understanding of Messianic anticipation of the original recipients of the oracles of God: the Nation of Israel. While there is a sea of literature surrounding these works, it is my recommendation that one desiring to know more just read the works themselves. The examination of these works confirm the supremacy, reliability, and accuracy of God's word: the Bible. Or as Proverbs 21:30 puts it:

> There is no wisdom or understanding
> Or counsel against the LORD.

Resources to Consider

- The Messiah Texts: Jewish Legends of Three Thousand Years by Raphael Patai. Wayne State University Press (December 1, 1988)
- The Old Testament Pseudepigrapha (Two Volumes) by James H. Charlesworth. Hendrickson Publishers. (June 2016.)
- The Apocrypha and Pseudepigrapha of the Old Testament in English: With Introduction and critical and explanatory notes to the several books (Two Volumes) by R.H. Charles. (not as high quality…but often can be found cheaper!)
- The Meaning of the Dead Sea Scrolls: Their Significance for Understanding the Bible, Judaism, Jesus, and Christianity by James VanderKam and Peter Flint. HarperOne (October 12, 2004).
- The Zondervan Handbook of Biblical Archaeology by Randall Price. Zondervan Academic (November 28, 2017)

The Houses of God

By Daniel E. Woodhead, Ph.D.

Introduction

God wants to be with His people on earth, and commanded different structures to be built to do this. His first structure was the portable Tabernacle that the Jews carried with them during the 40 years of wandering, and into the settlement days of their time in the Promised Land. Next came the First Temple built by King Solomon in Jerusalem as a permanent house of the Lord. After that was destroyed, the Second Temple was initially rebuilt by Zerubbabel and others in Jerusalem and enlarged by King Herod. That too was destroyed in 70 A.D. A Third Temple will be built for use during the Great Tribulation, which will also be destroyed. The final and most magnificent Fourth Temple will be built by and for King Jesus to rule in during the Millennial/Messianic Kingdom.

The Tabernacle

The Tabernacle, and later the Temple, are important for it was here the High Priest and other priests carried out their work to bring God to the people. The first dwelling for God's Presence (in Hebrew, "presence" is the word *Shekinah*) in the world was in the Sanctuary of the Tabernacle. (The Hebrew word for tabernacle is *Mishkan*). The Tabernacle accompanied the Jews on their journeys in the desert as they traveled from Mount Sinai to the Land of Israel. The Shekinah glory came into the Tabernacle and resided in the inner most chamber called the Holy of Holies. The High Priest would meet with God there once a year on *Yom Kippor*, the day of Atonement, to pray for the forgiveness of his sins and the Children of Israel's sins.

Moses was commanded to make a tabernacle for Him to dwell in on the earth, and it was to be patterned after the perfect Tabernacle in Heaven:

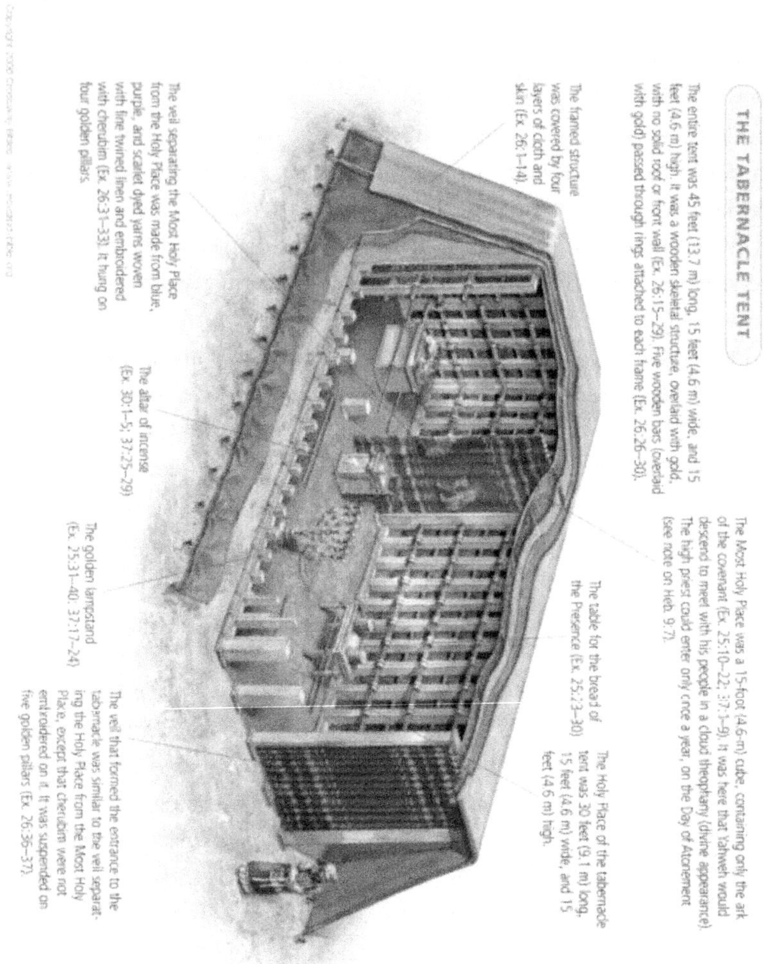

THE TABERNACLE TENT
The entire tent was 45 feet (13.7 m) long, 15 feet (4.6 m) wide, and 15 feet (4.6 m) high. It was a wooden skeletal structure, overlaid with gold, with no solid roof or front wall (Ex. 26:15–29). Five wooden bars (overlaid with gold) passed through rings attached to each frame (Ex. 26:26–30).
The Most Holy Place was a 15-foot (4.6-m) cube, containing only the ark of the covenant (Ex. 25:10–22; 37:1–9). It was here that Yahweh would descend to meet with his people in a cloud theophany (divine appearance). The high priest could enter only once a year, on the Day of Atonement (see note on Heb. 9:7).
The framed structure was covered by four layers of cloth and skin (Ex. 26:1–14).
The table for the bread of the Presence (Ex. 25:23–30)
The Holy Place of the tabernacle tent was 30 feet (9.1 m) long, 15 feet (4.6 m) wide, and 15 feet (4.6 m) high.
The veil separating the Most Holy Place from the Holy Place was made from blue, purple, and scarlet dyed yarns woven with fine twined linen and embroidered with cherubim (Ex. 26:31–33). It hung on four golden pillars.
The altar of incense (Ex. 30:1–5; 37:25–29)
The golden lampstand (Ex. 25:31–40; 37:17–24)
The veil that formed the entrance to the tabernacle was similar to the veil separating the Holy Place from the Most Holy Place, except that cherubim were not embroidered on it. It was suspended on five golden pillars (Ex. 26:36–37).

Figure 1: Tabernacle Cutaway from divinerevleations.info

> [8]And let them make me a sanctuary, that I may dwell among them. [9]According to all that I show thee, the pattern of the tabernacle, and the pattern of all the furniture thereof, even so shall ye make it (Ex. 25:8–9).[117]

Everything from the structure to the implements was to be made in all respects exactly according to the view, or images, Moses received from God. Moses then communicated these instructions and directions to the workmen. This was not to be made as an impression of the pattern, but an exact replica, or a perfect model of the patterns impressed on the mind of Moses. The image below one conception of is how the Tabernacle looked.

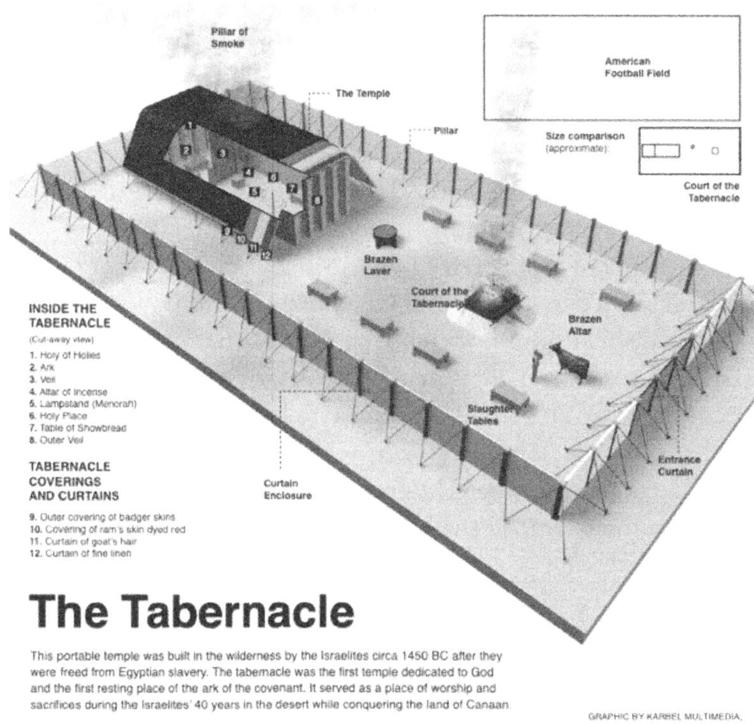

Figure 1 The Tabernacle from LOGOS Software

---

[117] Unless otherwise noted, all scripture references in this chapter are quoted from the ASV 1901.

After the Jews entered the land of Israel, the Tabernacle stood in Gilgal for 14 years. Afterwards the Tabernacle, including the ark, was moved into a permanent structure at Shiloh. This structure was erected with the same dimensions as the Tabernacle in the desert. In contrast to the original Tabernacle, which had wooden walls, the building erected at Shiloh was stone.

The First Temple

The next step was the construction of the First Temple in Jerusalem by King Solomon that replaced the Tabernacle at Shiloh and was to be a permanent building. Solomon was chosen to do this, not King David (2 Sam. 7:1– 17):

> [1]And Hiram king of Tyre sent his servants unto Solomon; for he had heard that they had anointed him king in the room of his father: for Hiram was ever a lover of David. [2]And Solomon sent to Hiram, saying, [3]Thou knowest how that David my father could not build a house for the name of Jehovah his God for the wars which were about him on every side, until Jehovah put them under the soles of his feet. [4]But now Jehovah my God hath given me rest on every side; there is neither adversary, nor evil occurrence. [5]And, behold, I purpose to build a house for the name of Jehovah my God, as Jehovah spake unto David my father, saying, Thy son, whom I will set upon thy throne in thy room, he shall build the house for my name. (1 Ki. 5:1–5)

Construction of the Temple began about 960 B.C.

> [1]And it came to pass in the four hundred and eightieth year after the children of Israel were come out of the land of Egypt, in the fourth year of Solomon's reign over Israel, in

the month Ziv, which is the second month, that he began to build the house of Jehovah (1 Ki. 6:1).

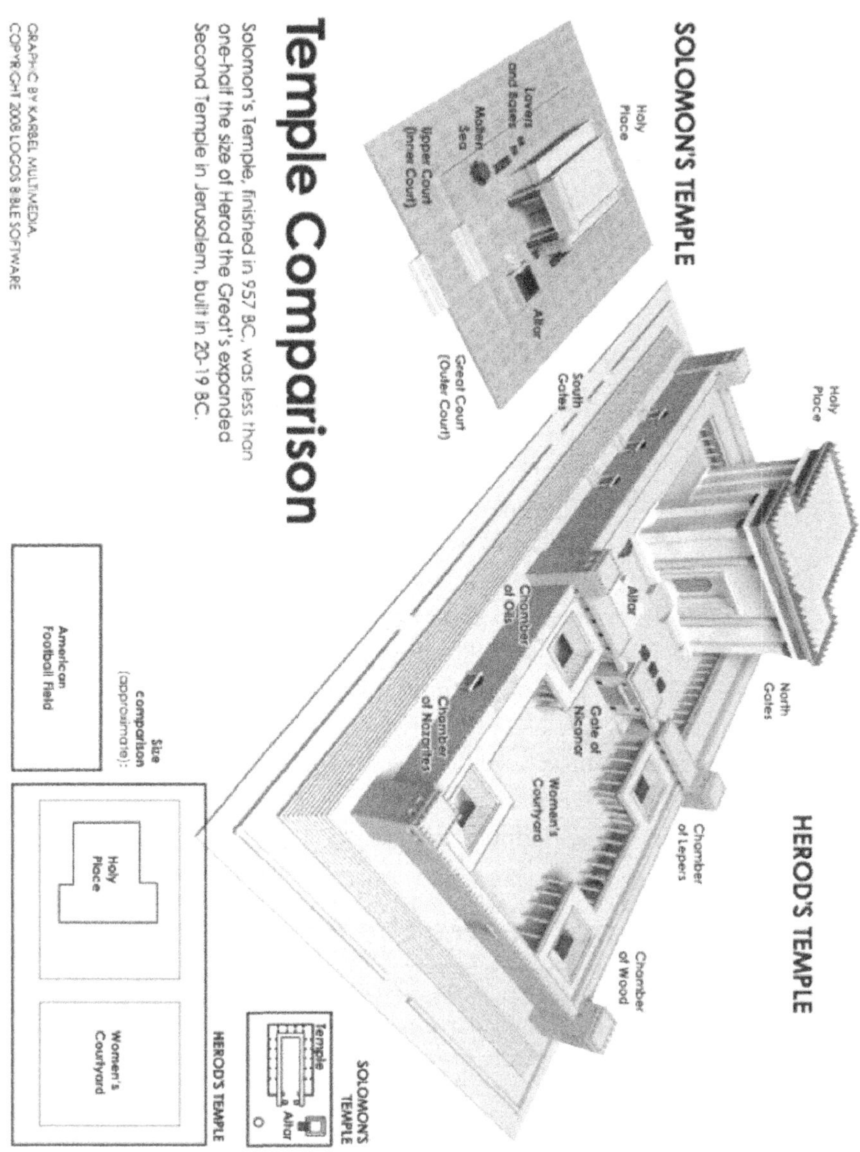

Figure 2 Herod's Temple from LOGOS Software

Among the differences between the Temple and the previous Tabernacle was an increase in the size of the altar and an increase in the size of the Temple building. The construction was completed in seven years, the number of God indicating completeness:

> [37]In the fourth year was the foundation of the house of Jehovah laid, in the month Ziv. [38]And in the eleventh year, in the month Bul, which is the eighth month, was the house finished throughout all the parts thereof, and according to all the fashion of it. So was he seven years in building it (1 Ki. 6:37– 38).

God's Glory Enters the Temple When King Solomon Conducted the Opening Ceremonies:

> [1]Now when Solomon had made an end of praying, the fire came down from heaven, and consumed the burnt-offering and the sacrifices; and the glory of Jehovah filled the house. [2]And the priests could not enter into the house of Jehovah, because the glory of Jehovah filled Jehovah's house. [3]And all the children of Israel looked on, when the fire came down, and the glory of Jehovah was upon the house; and they bowed themselves with their faces to the ground upon the pavement, and worshipped, and gave thanks unto Jehovah, saying, For, he is good; for his lovingkindness endureth for ever (2 Chron. 7:1–3).

The Lord Leaves the First Temple

The Jews greatly sinned. This caused the Lord to leave the Temple in 586 B.C. when He brought the Babylonians into Jerusalem to sack the Temple, and punish the nation Israel for turning against Him:

> [36] Jehovah said moreover unto me: Son of man, wilt thou judge Oholah and Oholibah? then declare unto them their abominations. [37] For they have committed adultery, and

> blood is in their hands; and with their idols have they committed adultery; and they have also caused their sons, whom they bare unto me, to pass through the fire unto them to be devoured (Ezek. 23:36–37).

The Lord begins this concluding section to the twenty-third chapter of the book of Ezekiel with an arraignment of the nation Israel. The central theme of Israel' sins against God had been discussed in chapters 20 to 23. Ezekiel is instructed to refer to the Northern Kingdom of Israel as the prostitute "*Oholah*" and the Southern Kingdom of Judah as the harlot "*Oholibah*", against whom formal charges are brought for their "*abominations*". The general crime against God is spiritual adultery committed by the nation Israel for their behavior as a prostitute instead of a loving wife. They prostituted themselves to the pagan cults, and were guilty of seven detestable practices listed in verses 36–37 including:

- Desecration of the Sabbath
- Desecration of the Temple
- Making forbidden foreign alliances
- Committing adultery
- Engaging in innocent bloodshed
- Committing child sacrifice
- Idolatry

So, the verdict is reached in this section of Scripture and the sentence is given for execution in chapter Ezekiel 24:1–27. Jehovah God leads Ezekiel to the inner court of the Temple to witness more abominations of the Jewish religious leaders. These corruptions were the worst Ezekiel ever saw.

> 16 And he brought me into the inner court of Jehovah's house; and behold, at the door of the temple of Jehovah, between the porch and the altar, were about five and twenty men, with their backs toward the temple of

Jehovah, and their faces toward the east; and they were worshipping the sun toward the east (Ezek. 8:16).

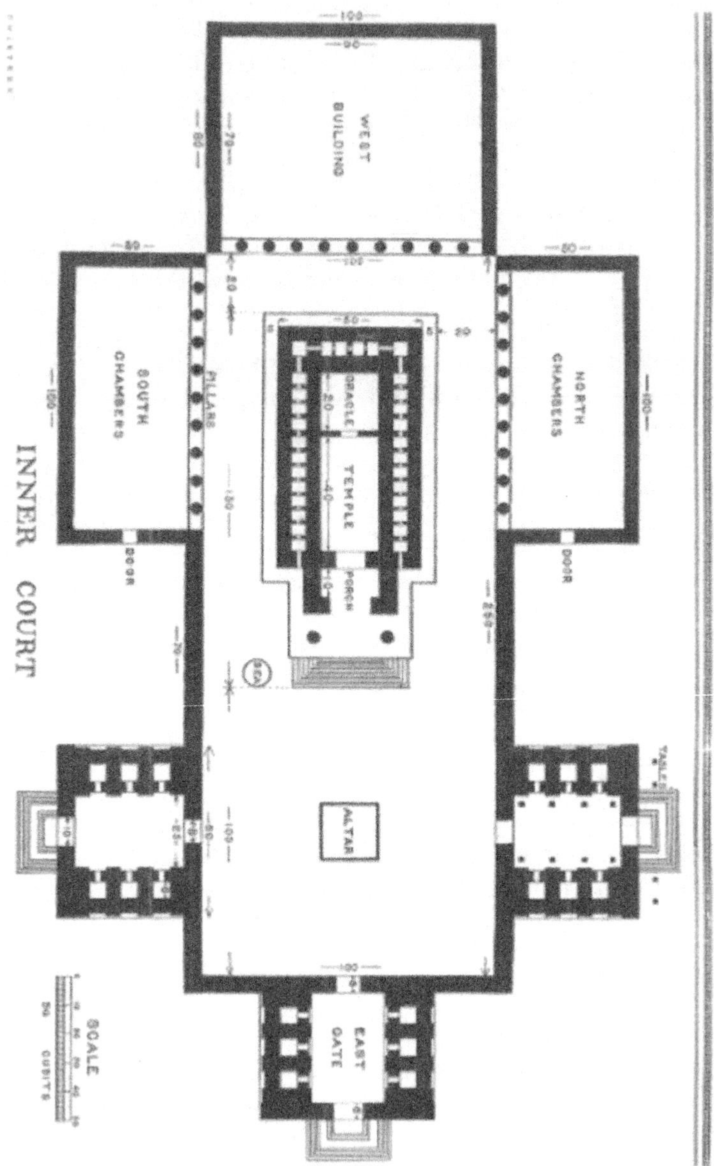

Figure 3 Image from Imgarcade.com-online image arcade Temple of Solomon

These men were probably twenty-five priests located between the covered entrance and the altar, with their backs to the Temple and their faces toward the sun. They were worshipping the sun, which they knew of from their days in Egypt, and now brought sun worship into God's Temple. Moses warned against these practices (Dt. 4:19). In attempting to avoid this, the Lord established the position of the sanctuary in such way so the entrance was facing west. In this configuration, those entering the Sanctuary would be facing the Holy of Holies with their back to the sun in the east. These twenty-five men had defied the Lord, faced the east, and bowed down to it in obeisance. In this way they were showing their contempt for the Temple of the God, and Him as well. Some Jewish interpreters see this act of defiance being carried out by the twenty-five defecating toward the Temple in obscene insolence as they bent over. They had uncovered themselves and evacuated downwards toward the Temple. (Eisenmann and Sherman, 1977, 167) The Jewish interpreters translate the Hebrew word *meeshtachvtem* as "bowing down *destructively*", not worshipping respectfully.

The sense of defiance toward God is apparent, which is why this particular abomination is the worst one of the seven listed above. The downward slide is clear for Israel. They had descended into idol worship, with its attendant sexual immorality and defiance to God. The New Testament letter of I John writes to the Church, "*My little children, guard yourselves from idols* "(I Jn. 5:21). This makes it apparent that it can happen to us if we do not heed the Word of God and become ensnared by the things of this world. Many churches have fallen victim to this as they move away from the Word of God and promote worldly practices. Consider the quote from Kent Dobson, pastor of Mars Hill Church in Grand Rapids, Michigan upon resigning:

> "I have always been and I'm still drawn to the very edges of religion and faith and God," Dobson said. "I've said a few times that I don't even know if we know what we mean by God anymore. That's the edges of faith. That's the thing that pulls me. I'm not really drawn to the center. I'm

not drawn to the orthodox or the mainstream or the status quo." (Vande Bunte, 11/23/2015)

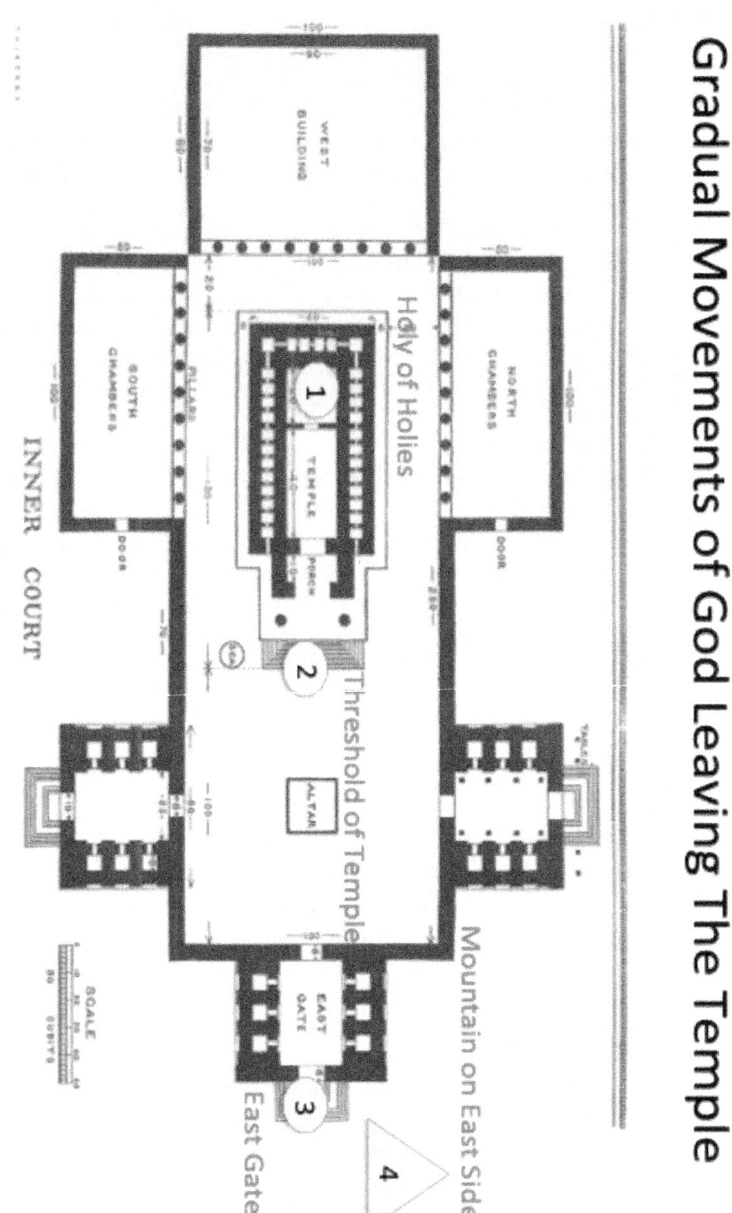

Cherubim Movement

God's presence left the Temple before the sentence was executed. All was set in motion to move God out of the Temple due to the sin of the religious leaders.

> [15]And the cherubim mounted up: this is the living creature
> that I saw by the river Chebar. [16]And when the cherubim
> went, the wheels went beside them; and when the cherubim
> lifted up their wings to mount up from the earth, the
> wheels also turned not from beside them. [17]When they
> stood, these stood; and when they mounted up, these
> mounted up with them: for the spirit of the living creature
> was in them (Ezek. 10:15–17).

The cherubim went in, the wheels went beside them in perfect unison. Upon command, the cherubim began lifting the Shekinah Glory up from the Temple The mighty wings of the cherubim lifted the Golden Chariot and the Lord up from the earth, and the wheels never swerved from their side. When the cherubim stood, the wheels stood. The energizing Spirit was in everything associated with this vision. The Glory of the Lord departed from the threshold of the Temple. Then in Ezekiel's sight the cherubim mounted up from the earth.

Jehovah Moves Out of the Temple

> [18]And the glory of Jehovah went forth from over the
> threshold of the house, and stood over the
> cherubim. [19]And the cherubim lifted up their wings, and
> mounted up from the earth in my sight when they went
> forth, and the wheels beside them: and they stood at the
> door of the east gate of Jehovah's house; and the glory of
> the God of Israel was over them above (Ezek. 10:18–19).

This was the second stage of the various ascensions as He left from the Holy of Holies. The Lord mounted His Golden Chariot in the Holy of Holies, went to the threshold and then upon His magnificent vehicle, stood over the east gate. It is important to note that God is not one with the Chariot, but above it, and the cherubim and chariot are obedient to Him as His need dictates. As God moved from The Holy of Holies upon the Chariot it moved Him to the threshold of the Temple, and then to the outer side of the east gate. The Glory is the same as seen before:

> [20]This is the living creature that I saw under the God of Israel by the river Chebar; and I knew that they were cherubim. [21]Every one had four faces, and every one four wings; and the likeness of the hands of a man was under their wings. [22]And as for the likeness of their faces, they were the faces which I saw by the river Chebar, their appearances and themselves; they went every one straight forward (Ezek. 10:20–22).

Thus, gradually, in solemn majesty, the Glory of the Lord, which had dwelt visibly in the Temple in the midst of His people, was departing. Verse 22 of chapter 11 connects with verse 19 of chapter 10. The complete departure of the Glory of the Lord from the midst of the city is recorded there. God moves to an unnamed mountain on the east side of the Temple. The diagram below numbers the progression of God leaving the First Temple.

The Glory has not abandoned Israel, for it will return: *"And the Glory of the Lord came into the house by the way of the gate whose front was toward the east"* (Ezek. 43:4). It will return in the same way as it departed. And that will be when the King, our Lord, comes back to earth again. At that time, the Glory will cover Israel and Jerusalem (Isa. 4:5; 60:1), and the knowledge of it will cover the earth as the waters cover the deep. This is the Millennial Temple, or Fourth Temple, where once again the Glory of God will inhabit the Temple.

What Ezekiel saw here is the same that he saw in chapter one during his first vision. The despair he senses with the Shekinah Glory departing the Temple is relieved in the chapter forty-three visions when Christ returns. The fact is God will never abandon His Chosen People:

> [44]And yet for all that, when they are in the land of their enemies, I will not reject them, neither will I abhor them, to destroy them utterly, and to break my covenant with them; for I am Jehovah their God; [45]but I will for their sakes remember the covenant of their ancestors, whom I brought forth out of the land of Egypt in the sight of the nations, that I might be their God: I am Jehovah (Lev. 26:44–45).

> [3]that then Jehovah thy God will turn thy captivity, and have compassion upon thee, and will return and gather thee from all the peoples, whither Jehovah thy God hath scattered thee. [4]If any of thine outcasts be in the uttermost parts of heaven, from thence will Jehovah thy God gather thee, and from thence will he fetch thee: [5]and Jehovah thy God will bring thee into the land which thy fathers possessed, and thou shalt possess it; and he will do thee good, and multiply thee above thy fathers (Dt. 30:3–5).

God corrects Israel, and His presence leaves the Temple, but He takes up residence at the unnamed mountain on the east side of the Temple. He is still near to them.

> [1]But now thus saith Jehovah that created thee, O Jacob, and he that formed thee, O Israel: Fear not, for I have redeemed thee; I have called thee by thy name, thou art mine. [2]When thou passest through the waters, I will be with thee; and through the rivers, they shall not overflow thee: when thou walkest through the fire, thou shalt not be burned, neither shall the flame kindle upon thee. [3]For I am Jehovah thy God, the Holy One of Israel, thy Saviour; I have given Egypt as thy ransom, Ethiopia and Seba in thy stead. [4]Since thou hast been precious in my sight, and honorable, and I have loved thee; therefore will I give men in thy stead, and peoples instead of thy life. [5]Fear not; for I am with thee: I will bring thy seed from the east, and gather thee from the west; [6]I will say to the north, Give up; and to the south, Keep not back; bring my sons from far, and my daughters from the end of the earth; [7]every one that is

called by my name, and whom I have created for my glory, whom I have formed, yea, whom I have made (Isa. 43:1–7).

Jesus says the same thing to the Church. He will never leave us (Mt. 28:20; Heb. 13:5).

Dating the Judgment

> [1]Again, in the ninth year, in the tenth month, in the tenth day of the month, the word of Jehovah came unto me, saying, [2] Son of man, write thee the name of the day, even of this selfsame day: the king of Babylon drew close unto Jerusalem this selfsame day [3] And utter a parable unto the rebellious house, and say unto them (Ezek. 24:1–2).

This verse started with Ezekiel stating the date this message from God was given. On January 15, 588 B.C. of the Gregorian, also known as the western calendar, this message was received by Ezekiel. This most significant event was also recorded in three other places in the Old Testament:

> [1]And it came to pass in the ninth year of his reign, in the tenth month, in the tenth day of the month, that Nebuchadnezzar king of Babylon came, he and all his army, against Jerusalem, and encamped against it; and they built forts against it round about (2 Ki. 25:1).

> [1] In the ninth year of Zedekiah king of Judah, in the tenth month, came Nebuchadnezzar king of Babylon and all his army against Jerusalem, and besieged it (Jer. 39:1).

> [4]And it came to pass in the ninth year of his (Zedekiah) reign, in the tenth month, in the tenth day of the month, that Nebuchadnezzar king of Babylon came, he and all his army, against Jerusalem, and encamped against it; and they built forts against it round about (Jer. 53:4).

This was the long-prophesied day when the Babylonian army under Nebuchadnezzar set their siege against Jerusalem. This started two and a half years before the destruction of the Temple in 586 B.C. So ends the first Temple.

The Babylonian Captivity Ends

One hundred and seventy-five years before Cyrus was born, the Lord foretells that Cyrus the Mede, His servant, will conquer Babylon and deliver the Chosen People back to the Land:

> [1]Thus saith Jehovah to his anointed, to Cyrus, whose right hand I have holden, to subdue nations before him, and I will loose the loins of kings; to open the doors before him, and the gates shall not be shut: [2]I will go before thee, and make the rough places smooth; I will break in pieces the doors of brass, and cut in sunder the bars of iron (Isa. 45:1–2).

A Timeline of These Events:

549–530 B.C.	Rise to world-rule of Cyrus the Persian.
549 B.C.	Cyrus unites Persia and Media
546 B.C.	Cyrus conquers Lydia
539 B.C.	Cyrus conquers Babylon (this ends the Chaldean Empire)

The Persian Empire (539–331 B.C.) and the Restoration of Judah

538 B.C.	Edict of Cyrus permitting Jewish repatriation of Judah (Ez. 1)
537–536 B.C.	Return of 49,897 Jews to Jerusalem (Ez. 2; Neh. 7)
536 B.C.	Altar rebuilt and sacrifices offered (seventh month)
535 B.C.	Work on temple started, but then stopped (Ez. 3:1–4)
535–520 B.C.	Hardships, economic depression in Jerusalem; people forget the temple and selfishly concentrate on their own needs (Hag. 1, 2)
530 B.C.	The death of Cyrus

530–522 B.C.	Reign of Cyrus' son, Cambyses II, who conquered Egypt
522–486 B.C.	Darius I, The Great, saved the empire from civil war, erected the Behistun Inscription and was friendly to the Jews
520 B.C.	Darius confirms the decree of Cyrus and aids in the construction of the Jewish temple in Jerusalem (Ez. 6:1–14)
520 B.C.	**6th month (September–October) 1st day of the month,** Haggai's first sermon (Hag. 1:3–11)
520 B.C.	**6th month, 24th day,** Haggai's second sermon (Hag. 1:12–15)
520 B.C.	**7th month (October–November), 1st day,** Haggai's third sermon (Hag. 2:1–9)
520 B.C.	**8th month, (November–December), 1st day,** Zechariah's opening sermon (Zech. 1:1–6)
520 B.C.	**8th month, 24th day,** Haggai's last sermons (Hag. 2:10–23)
520 B.C.	**11th month (February–March) 24th day,** Zechariah's eight-night visions (Zech. 1:7–6:8)
520 B.C.	**11th month, 24th or 25th day**, the symbolic crowning of Joshua prefiguring Messiah King-Priest
518 B.C.	**Ninth month (December–January) 4th day,** delegation from Bethel; Zechariah's message of repentance and promised blessing (Zech. 7–8)
516 B.C.	**12th month (March-April) 3rd day,** completion and dedication of the temple (Ez. 6:15)
490 B.C.	Darius I's campaign against Greece, Defeat at Marathon
486–465 B.C.	Xerxes I (Ahasuerus) husband of Esther (Esth. 2:16), reigns
480 B.C.	Persians defeated at Thermopylae and Salamis by the Greeks
478 B.C.	Esther becomes queen
465–424 B.C.	Reign of Artaxerxes I
458 B.C.	Ezra returns to Israel (some scholars date this event later)
445 B.C.	Artaxerxes I authorizes Nehemiah to restore Jerusalem's walls

445–432 B.C.	Malachi's ministry (approximate dates)
424–423 B.C.	Xerxes II
423–404 B.C.	Darius II
404–358 B.C.	Artaxerxes II
358–338 B.C.	Artaxerxes III
338–336 B.C.	Arses
336–331 B.C.	Darius III Defeated by Alexander of Macedon

During the reign of Darius the First, the prophet Daniel receives a vision of the end of the desolations of Jerusalem:

> 1In the first year of Darius the son of Ahasuerus, of the seed of the Medes, who was made king over the realm of the Chaldeans, 2in the first year of his reign I, Daniel, understood by the books the number of the years whereof the word of Jehovah came to Jeremiah the prophet, for the accomplishing of the desolations of Jerusalem, even seventy years (Dan. 9:1–2).

THE SECOND TEMPLE

God chooses the correct new High Priest for the next Temple:

> 5And I said, Let them set a clean mitre upon his head. So they set a clean mitre upon his head, and clothed him with garments; and the angel of Jehovah was standing by. 6And the angel of Jehovah protested unto Joshua, saying, 7Thus saith Jehovah of hosts: If thou wilt walk in my ways, and if thou wilt keep my charge, then thou also shalt judge my house, and shalt also keep my courts, and I will give thee a place of access among these that stand by (Zech. 3:5–10).

Now, the prophet Zechariah describes the events in the Holy Supreme Court. Interjecting himself into the event, Zechariah clearly says to the attending angelic host to "*set a clean mitre upon his head*". He is referring to Joshua the High Priest who is in the court, but dressed in filthy clothes. The Hebrew word for High Priest is *Kohen Gadol.* The filthy clothes Joshua is wearing represents the sin that the nation Israel has committed, which resulted in their persecution by the God of the Universe. This symbolic act of God forgiving their national sin is also going to happen on a future day at the end of the Great Tribulation when the entire nation will believe in Jesus as their Messiah (Romans 11:26).

Here we see the crowning of the High Priest's change to festive clothes with the "*mitre*", or turban. This capping signified his office, so to speak, being upon his forehead. We can assume that a golden plate that was attached to the headband of the mitre, on which was written "*holiness to the Lord*" (Ex. 28:38). This was a special command of the Lord when the original garments of the High Priest were ordered (Ex. 28:36-39). Now Joshua is appropriately dressed for his office. "*Jehovah of hosts*" now charges him to behave in such a way so that he would be emanating holiness. This holiness would be to represent the return to God of the redeemed Chosen People. The High Priest's office had become extremely sinful, and therefore unable to render God's holiness to the Jewish nation. With Joshua receiving the "*mitre*", he acknowledges he is willing and able to execute the office of the High Priest to the nation so they can be provided with God's holiness through this earthly assigned intercessor. The high degree of significance of this event must not be missed.

The books of Ezra and Nehemiah cover the period from the fall of Babylon in 539 B.C. to the second half of the 5th century B.C. They tell of the successive missions to Jerusalem of Zerubbabel, Ezra, and Nehemiah and their efforts to restore the worship of the God of Israel, and to create a purified Jewish community. In Ezra 1–6, God moves the heart of Cyrus to commission Sheshbazzar (whose other name is Zerubbabel) "the prince of Judah", to rebuild the Temple. 40,000 exiles return to Jerusalem led by Zerubbabel and Joshua as the newly commissioned High Priest. The Second Temple was enhanced by Herod the Great.

Herod's Enlargement

Reconstruction and expansion of the Temple under Herod began with a massive expansion of the Temple Mount. Herod's work on the Temple is dated from about 20/19 B.C. until 12/11 or 10 B.C. Religious worship and Temple rituals continued during the construction process.

The prophet Daniel received a prophecy of the destruction of the Second Temple:

> [24]Seventy weeks are decreed upon thy people and upon thy holy city, to finish transgression, and to make an end of sins, and to make reconciliation for iniquity, and to bring in everlasting righteousness, and to seal up vision and prophecy, and to anoint the most holy. [25]Know therefore and discern, that from the going forth of the commandment to restore and to build Jerusalem unto the anointed one, the prince, shall be seven weeks, and threescore and two weeks: it shall be built again, with street and moat, even in troublous times. [26]And after the threescore and two weeks shall the anointed one be cut off, and shall have nothing: and the people of the prince that shall come shall destroy the city and the sanctuary; and the end thereof shall be with a flood, and even unto the end shall be war; desolations are determined. [27]And he shall make a firm covenant with many for one week: and in the midst of the week he shall cause the sacrifice and the oblation to cease; and upon the wing of abominations shall come one that maketh desolate; and even unto the full end, and that determined, shall wrath be poured out upon the desolate (Dan. 9:24–27).

The purposes of this prophecy were:

1. To finish the transgression. In this first purpose, sin is to come under control so that it will no longer flourish, specifically, Israel's sin of the rejection of the Messiahship of Jesus. Israel's national sin is now to be firmly restrained and brought to completion. The same point is brought out in Isaiah 59:20 and

Romans 11:26. The first purpose, then, is to end Israel's national transgression, which was the rejection of the Messiahship of Jesus.

2 To make an end of sins. The point in this purpose is that, while there may be sin among the Gentile nations, in the Kingdom there will be no sin in Israel. This very same truth is taught in Isaiah 27:9; Ezekiel 36:25–27; 37:23; and Romans 11:27. This is also the point of the New Covenant in Jeremiah 31:31–34, where Jeremiah clearly predicts the day will come when all Israel's sins will be removed and all Israel will be saved, from the least to the greatest.

3 To make reconciliation for iniquity. The program of the Seventy Sevens is a cleansing of Israel that will include the removal of all three things: first, the national sin of rejecting His Messiahship; second, sinning daily; and third, dealing with the sin nature itself.

4 To bring in an age of righteousness. The fourth purpose is to bring in an age of righteousness to establish the Kingdom. Daniel thought the Kingdom would be set up immediately after the seventy years of captivity. Now he is told that this will occur not after seventy years, but after seventy sevens of years or 490 years.

5 To cause a cessation of prophecy. The fifth purpose of the Seventy Sevens is to cause a cessation of both oral and written prophecy, because the program of the Seventy Sevens will contain the final fulfillment of all prophecies. The function of all prophecies will cease at the Second Coming of the Messiah.

6 To anoint the most holy place. The most holy place is not the First Temple of Solomon, nor the Second Temple of Zerubbabel, and certainly not the Third Temple of the Great Tribulation. Rather, it is the Fourth Temple, the Temple of the Messianic Kingdom, built by the Lord Himself, and it will be anointed as part of the program of Seventy Sevens.

7 The starting point of the Seventy Sevens. Daniel 9:24 already stated that the program of the Seventy Sevens concerns not only the Jewish people, but also the Jewish city of Jerusalem. Now in Daniel 9:25a, he is told that the Seventy Sevens will begin with a decree, one that involves the rebuilding of Jerusalem.

8 The first Seven Sevens. Daniel 9:25bstates the first subdivision, the seven sevens, is a total of forty-nine years and refers to the forty-nine-year period that it took to rebuild Jerusalem. In speaking of the rebuilding of Jerusalem, it speaks of the city as being "*built again, with street and moat, even in troublous times*" The first subdivision of the Seventy Sevens, then, is the seven sevens, or forty-nine years, during which time Jerusalem was rebuilt. Only after forty-nine years was the rebuilding process brought to completion.

9 The Sixty-Two Sevens or Four Hundred Thirty-Four Years. Combining seven sevens and sixty-two sevens gives a total of sixty-nine sevens. Or combining forty-nine years with 434 years gives a total of 483 years. A total of 483 years will transpire from the time that the decree is issued until the coming of the Messiah, "*the prince*". Hence the first 483 years of the 490-year period came to an end with the First Coming of the Messiah.

10 The events between the Sixty-Ninth and the Seventieth Sevens. Daniel 9:26 states that while there was no gap of time between the first subdivision and the second subdivision of the Seventy Sevens, there is a gap of time between the second subdivision and the third subdivision. Verse 26 starts out: "*And after the threescore and two* [62] *weeks*", after the second subdivision, certain things must occur before the third subdivision begins in verse 27. When he says, "after the sixty-two sevens," he means after the conclusion of the second subdivision of the Seventy Sevens and before the beginning of the third subdivision of the Seventy Sevens. This phrase clearly shows that a gap of time exists between the second and third subdivisions, that is, between the sixty-ninth seven and the seventieth seven. In this gap of time three events are to occur.

11 The Messiah would be killed. It is not "*the prince that shall come* "who will destroy the city and the Temple, but rather, "*the people of the prince that shall come*". The point of that second phrase in verse 26 is that the nationality of "*the people*" and "*the prince that shall come*" are one and the same. "*The prince that shall come*" in this context is the Antichrist of whom Daniel has already spoken of in chapters 7 and 8. By saying "*the prince,*" Daniel uses the article of previous reference, because he has spoken of him in the previous chapters. "*The prince that shall come*", which is still future,

is of the same nationality as "*the people*" who will destroy the city and the Temple. After the Messiah is cut off, the city and the Temple will be destroyed.

12 The destruction of Jerusalem and the Temple. This occurred in A.D. 70, forty years after the death of the Messiah. It is known from history who "*the people*" "*The people*" who destroyed the city and the Temple in A.D. 70 were the Gentiles of Rome, the Romans. Since the Antichrist must be of the same nationality as the people who destroyed the city and the Temple, it is this verse that shows that the Antichrist will be a Gentile of Roman origin. Then he states: "*and the end thereof shall be with a flood*," meaning that the end of Jerusalem and the Temple shall be the result of "*a flood*." Whenever the figure of a flood is used symbolically, it always is a symbol of a military invasion. Jerusalem was destroyed by a Roman military invasion, first under Vespasian and then under Titus.

Jesus affirmed the destruction of the Second Temple

Jesus was taken the Second Temple by His parents on the eighth day of His life for His circumcision. This was the last time the Shekinah Glory entered the Second Temple (Lk. 2:22–38). Years later, during the last week of His life, Jesus said the Temple would be destroyed:

> 1And Jesus went out from the temple, and was going on his way; and his disciples came to him to show him the buildings of the temple. 2But he answered and said unto them, See ye not all these things? verily I say unto you, There shall not be left here one stone upon another, that shall not be thrown down (Mt. 24:1–2).

The Third Temple of the Great Tribulation

Several passages of Scripture indicate that the activities of the Antichrist involve a future Jewish Temple:

- Daniel 9:27 – The prince who is to come confirms a covenant for the duration of the 70th Week of Daniel. In the middle of the week, *"he shall bring an end to sacrifice and offering."* This implies a preexisting Temple within which sacrifice and offering had been taking place.
- Daniel 12:11 – The daily sacrifice will be taken away and the Abomination of Desolation is set up. The context indicates that this occurs during "a time of trouble, such as never was since there was a [Jewish] nation" (Dan. 12:1). A Temple must have been standing in which the daily sacrifices were being offered.
- Matthew 24:15 – Jesus predicted that the Abomination of Desolation would stand "in the holy place." This refers to a location within the Temple.
- 2 Thessalonians 2:4 – Paul indicated that one of the acts of "the man of sin" would be to exalt himself "above all that is called God or is worshiped, so that he sits as God *in the temple of God,*showing himself that he is God." [emphasis added]
- Revelation 11:1 – John is told to measure "the temple of God, the altar, and those who worship there." The context is during the Great Tribulation, prior to the return of Christ.

Implied Destruction of the Third Temple

Isaiah states the structure of the earth changes, and could be a cause of the Third Temple destruction:

> [19] The earth is utterly broken down, the earth is clean dissolved, the earth is moved exceedingly. [20] The earth shall reel to and fro like a drunkard, and shall be removed like a cottage; and the transgression thereof shall be heavy upon it; and it shall fall, and not rise again (Isa. 24:19–20 KJV).

One result of the Great Tribulation is the leveling of the earth surface through multiple earthquakes. Some of this occurs during the judgment of the bowls which follow after the judgment of the trumpets during the second half of the Great Tribulation:

> [17] And the seventh angel poured out his vial into the air; and there came a great voice out of the temple of heaven,

> from the throne, saying, It is done. [18] And there were voices, and thunders, and lightnings; and there was a great earthquake, such as was not since men were upon the earth, so mighty an earthquake, and so great. [19] And the great city was divided into three parts, and the cities of the nations fell: and great Babylon came in remembrance before God, to give unto her the cup of the wine of the fierceness of his wrath. [20] And every island fled away, and the mountains were not found. [21] And there fell upon men a great hail out of heaven, every stone about the weight of a talent: and men blasphemed God because of the plague of the hail; for the plague thereof was exceeding great (Rev. 16:17–21 KJV).

The pivotal event, which signals the mid-point of the Great Tribulation, is the Antichrist's takeover of the Jewish Temple. He breaks his covenant with the Jews and declares himself "The Almighty God". He also begins a serious persecution of the Jews, which will last for 1,260 days. The False Prophet sets up an inanimate image of the Antichrist in the Temple, and Satan causes it to become alive. The Antichrist is in control of the world for those 1,260 days, and then he will be killed:

> [11]And from the time that the continual burnt offering shall be taken away, and the abomination that maketh desolate set up, there shall be a thousand and two hundred and ninety days (Dan. 12:11).

The image stays in the Temple for additional thirty days. The desecration of the Jewish Temple lasts an additional thirty days beyond the end of the Great Tribulation, then it will be destroyed, which brings the Abomination of Desolation to an end. From this passage it appears that the Tribulation Temple will be finally destroyed after the end of the Great Tribulation.

The Millennial Fourth Temple on the Millennial Mountain

As result of the leveling of the earth' surface, the highest mountain on earth will be in Israel. The Lord spoke through the prophet Micah of His Millennial Mountain:

> [1]But in the latter days it shall come to pass, that the mountain of Jehovah's house shall be established on the top of the mountains, and it shall be exalted above the hills; and peoples shall flow unto it. [2]And many nations shall go and say, Come ye, and let us go up to the mountain of Jehovah, and to the house of the God of Jacob; and he will teach us of his ways, and we will walk in his paths. For out of Zion shall go forth the law, and the word of Jehovah from Jerusalem (Mic. 4:1–3).

Micah received nearly the same information as Isaiah which emphasizes its importance to the Lord. He also was privy to learn that the Millennial Mountain will be the highest, be exulted above all, and God's Law would proceed from it. It will be the center of the world's government activities. Ezekiel received the most information regarding the Millennial Mountain and the Fourth Temple that will be erected during that time.

The Location of the Temple

> [2]Of this there shall be for the holy place five hundred in length by five hundred in breadth, square round about; and fifty cubits for the suburbs thereof round about. [3]And of this measure shalt thou measure a length of five and twenty thousand, and a breadth of ten thousand: and in it shall be the sanctuary, which is most holy. [4]It is a holy portion of the land; it shall be for the priests, the ministers of the sanctuary, that come near to minister unto Jehovah; and it shall be a place for their houses, and a holy place for the sanctuary. [5]And five and twenty thousand in length, and ten thousand in breadth, shall be unto the Levites, the ministers

> of the house, for a possession unto themselves, for twenty chambers (Ezek. 45:2–5).

This very high mountain, the highest in the world, will itself have a fifty-mile square plateau on top (v. 1). This square plateau will be subdivided into three sections. The northern section (vv. 2–4) will be twenty miles by fifty miles, having in its center the Millennial Temple, which will be about one mile square. The rest of the area of the northern section will be reserved for the Zadokites to live. These are "*the priests, the ministers of the sanctuary, that come near to minister unto Jehovah*".

The central section (v. 5) will also be twenty miles by fifty miles and will be reserved for the members of the Tribe of Levi. Chapter forty-eight will explain their allotment and positioning in greater detail. The text of verse five cites specific buildings for the Levites who will care for the more mundane activities in the Temple. Referred to as "*for a possession unto themselves, for twenty chambers*", there is no explanation as to exactly how these chambers will be used. Instead of being scattered throughout Israel as before the captivity (Josh 21:1–42), they will now live close to the Temple where they will minister.

Millennial Jerusalem in the Southern Section

> 6And ye shall appoint the possession of the city five thousand broad, and five and twenty thousand long, side by side with the oblation of the holy portion: it shall be for the whole house of Israel. 7And whatsoever is for the prince shall be on the one side and on the other side of the holy oblation and of the possession of the city, in front of the holy oblation and in front of the possession of the city, on the west side westward, and on the east side eastward; and in length answerable unto one of the portions, from the west border unto the east border. 8In the land it shall be to him for a possession in Israel: and my princes shall no more oppress my people; but they shall give the land to the house of Israel according to their tribes (Ezek. 45:6–8).

The southern section (vv. 6–8) will be ten miles by fifty miles, the smallest of the three. The city of Millennial Jerusalem, which will be ten miles by ten miles square. The city proper will belong to all people not to any particular tribe. On either side of the city will be field areas, each measuring ten by twenty miles, for growing food. These areas will be overseen by the prince, the resurrected David, who will apportion the Land according to tribe, as detailed in chapter forty-eight. This section will be considered as ordinary (in the Hebrew "ordinary" is *chol*) because of the city and fields for produce for the people living in the city. This is different than the designation of the two northern

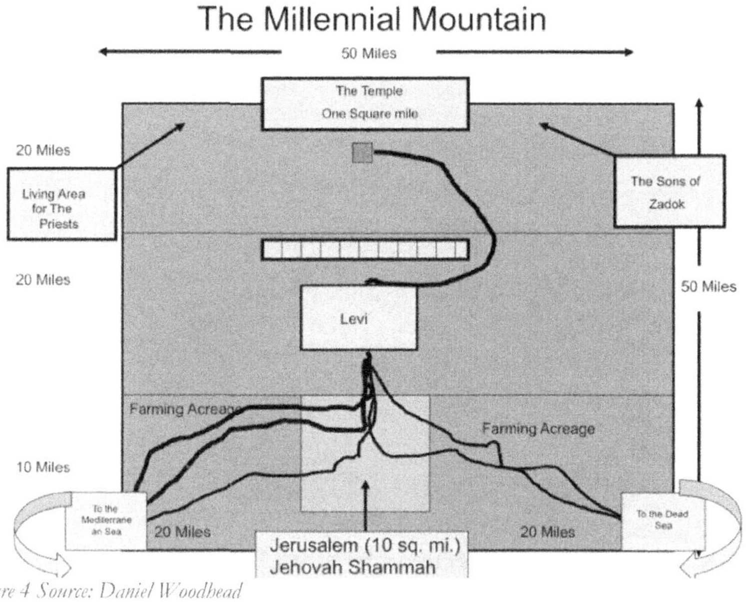

Figure 4 Source: Daniel Woodhead

sections that are called "holy" or "sanctified" (in the Hebrew, *kadosh*). Below is a diagram of the 3 sections:

God Promises a Sanctuary in Israel

27My tabernacle also shall be with them; and I will be their
God, and they shall be my people. 28And the nations shall
know that I am Jehovah that sanctifieth Israel, when my

sanctuary shall be in the midst of them for evermore (Ezek. 37:26–28).

During the Babylonian exile, God revealed a vision of the ultimate Millennial, or Messianic Temple, to the prophet Ezekiel. When the Jews returned from Babylon to build the Second Temple, they desired to build that structure in accordance with Ezekiel's prophecy but had difficulty comprehending all of its particulars. Therefore, they structured the building according to the plan of the First Temple, incorporating whatever innovations were clear to them that Ezekiel had envisioned.

God, in His Divine providence, is beginning to describe the home He is going to build for Himself on earth during the Messianic Kingdom:

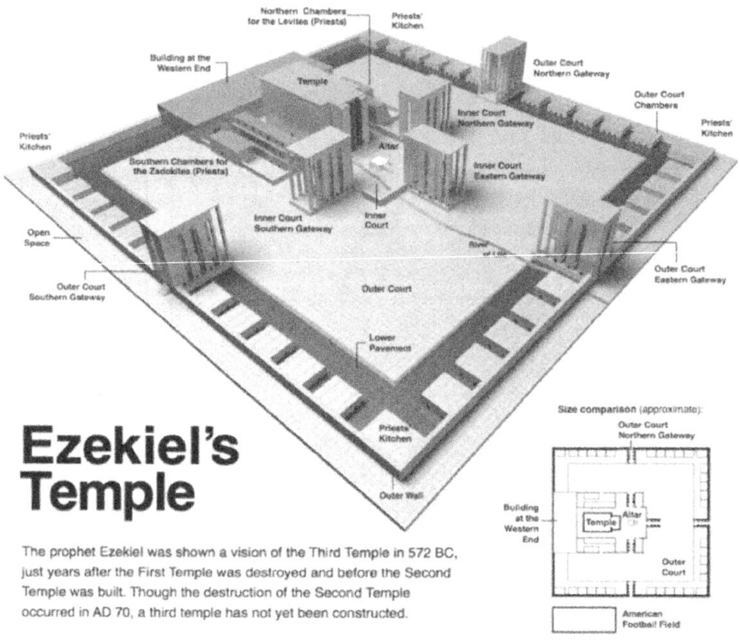

Figure 5 Millennial Temple from: LOGOS Software

[12]and speak unto him, saying, Thus speaketh Jehovah of hosts, saying, Behold, the man whose name is the Branch:

> and he shall grow up out of his place; and he shall build the temple of Jehovah; [13]even he shall build the temple of Jehovah; and he shall bear the glory, and shall sit and rule upon his throne; and he shall be a priest upon his throne; and the counsel of peace shall be between them both. [14]And the crowns shall be to Helem, and to Tobijah, and to Jedaiah, and to Hen the son of Zephaniah, for a memorial in the temple of Jehovah. [15]And they that are far off shall come and build in the temple of Jehovah; and ye shall know that Jehovah of hosts hath sent me unto you. And this shall come to pass, if ye will diligently obey the voice of Jehovah your God (Zech. 6:12–15).

This will be a period of time on the earth where Jesus Christ will be running the government of the earth from Jerusalem. His Temple will be the place in which He will be.

References

Eisemann, Rabbi Moshe, and Sherman, Rabbi Nosson. (1977). *Yechezkel: Translation and Commentary*. Brooklyn, NY: Mesorah Publications Ltd.

Vande Bunte, M. (November 23, 2015). "Rob Bell's successor at Mars Hill is stepping down." Retrieved from http://www.mlive.com/news/grandrapids/index.ssf/2015/11/rob_bells_ successor_at_mars_hi.html January, 2020.

About the Authors:

Jacob P. Heaton

Jacob P. Heaton and his wife Amanda Heaton live in Thornton, Colorado where they raise their three sons. Jacob is the pastor of Fellowship Bible Church (http://www.fbcedgewater.org) which serves the Denver metro area. In addition, Jacob is on staff at Fort Collins Bible College.

Jacob received his B.A. at Frontier School of the Bible in LaGrange, WY, and is currently pursuing a ThM at Chafer Theological Seminary and a M. Div. at Colorado Biblical University.

Bradley W. Maston

Brad and his family have served the Lord in many different capacities. He has worked teaching the Bible in South Korea, served outreach missions with at-risk youth, and has been a youth pastor to two Korean congregations. He received an MA in Biblical Theology at Channel Islands Bible College and Seminary and was mentored and built up at Holly Hills Bible Church. He completed his Ph.D. IN Jewish Studies at Scofield Bible Institute with a focus on Jewish Intertestamental Literature. Brad is passionate about the clear teaching of God's word and building up Christian leaders. He is a board member and adjunct professor at Chafer Theological Seminary. He is also an adjunct professor at Scofield Bible Institute. For nearly a decade, Brad has been involved in Camp Arete which has a mission of teaching and encouraging young believers in middle school and high school. Pastor Brad's messages can be heard daily on Grace Global Radio. He also heads the Fort Collins Bible Church Biblical Training Program which makes seminary-level education available to anyone accepted into the program entirely free of charge. Brad is also the founding President of the Fort Collins Bible College and professor of Bible Study Methods and Church History at that institution.

Benjamin Coleman

After graduating from Frontier School of the Bible with a Bachelor of Arts degree in Biblical Studies, Ben moved on to obtain both a Bachelor of Science degree in Business Administration and a Master of Accountancy degree from Colorado State University. He has served in several organizations, such as the Holland Rescue Mission and Frontier School of the Bible, gaining experience in nonprofit accounting and systems. Ben and his wife Holley have a passion for using their gifts in ways that grow them and others.

J. Morgan Arnold

J. Morgan Arnold (B.B.A, Texas A&M University) is a graduate student at Chafer Seminary. He has been the co-owner of a search engine marketing firm since 2013 and has worked at several Dallas advertising agencies as a marketing specialist since 2003. From 1994-2001, he served as a Director for the Union Gospel Mission of Seattle. For the past eight years, he has served as a men's Bible teacher for Bible Study Fellowship in Denton and Decatur, TX. He and his wife, Rocki, have been married for 30 years. They boast two grown children and two lazy Labrador retrievers.

Dr. Daniel Woodhead

Dr. Daniel E. Woodhead is a pastor of a Bible Church and President of Theology in Perspective. He is also the president of Scofield Biblical Institute and Theological Seminary. He has been a Bible teacher for more than twenty-five years. He earned his Ph.D. from Scofield seminary under Dr. Mal Couch and holds an MBA from the University of Detroit. He is a attended Hebrew University in Jerusalem and Hebrew College in Massachusetts. He has been a successful entrepreneur in the energy industry and is married with three children and two grandchildren.

Donald Thomas

Donald Thomas was raised on a farm in Southern Idaho with 6 siblings in a Christian environment. He attended the University of Idaho where he earned a Bachelor of Science degree. He served 2 ½ years in the Army with two years in Germany. He worked for the US Department of Agriculture for 27-years in Idaho, Washington, Minnesota, and Colorado. He then worked for an electrical engineering consulting firm in Fort Collins, Colorado for 13 ½ years and retired in 2012. He has been a member of Fort Collins Bible Church since 2001 where he received the Bible Basics Certificate. He completed the Contenders Discipleship Initiative sponsored by Village Missions, Dallas, Oregon. His ministry has focused on teaching God's Word to new believers and on the truthfulness of Scripture as confirmed by science. Born in 1946, he has experienced the evolution of the current worldview of religion. He has been married to Sharon since 1967 and they have a son and a daughter, five grandchildren and one great grandchild. He can be reached via email at don.thomas.1554@comcast.net.

E Dane Rogers

Dane is the pastor of Tacoma Grace Bible Church. After graduating from the University of Victoria, British Columbia, with a B.A. in Hispanic and Italian Studies, Dane moved to South Korea to teach elementary and middle school English at EiE, Korea University's preparatory academy. Dane continued his graduate studies (MBS) at Chafer Theological Seminary while living and working in Korea before returning to the USA in 2021 where he began pastoring at Tacoma Grace Bible Church in Washington State. Dane is now working toward his ThM at Chafer. Most recently, Dane has joined the faculty at Fort Collins Bible College. Bible study recordings and other study materials are available at edanerogers.com and tacomagracebc.org.

Randy Peterman

Randy is grateful for the grace of God every day of his life. He has been united as one to his wife Jessica for an absurd number of years. Randy and Jessica have two amazing daughters and, now, grandchildren! When he's not programming or thinking about theology he likes to collect hobbies and make people laugh. If you meet Randy he would like you to know he's a hugger.

Made in the USA
Columbia, SC
18 August 2023